THE NEW THINKER'S LIBRARY

General Editor: RAYMOND WILLIAMS

SOVEREIGNTY

SOVEREIGNTY

By
F. H. HINSLEY

LONDON
C. A. WATTS & CO. LTD.
1966

First published 1966

©
F. H. HINSLEY
1966

PRINTED IN GREAT BRITAIN IN THE CITY OF OXFORD AT THE ALDEN PRESS
36/613

PREFACE

It is difficult to avoid errors and uncertainties of fact or emphasis when writing a small book on a large subject. I have done what I could to reduce their number by being a burden on friends and colleagues in Cambridge, where I am particularly indebted to Mr. John Crook, Dr. Jack Goody, Dr. Clive Parry and Dr. Audrey Richards. Johns Hopkins University spurred me on by most kindly inviting me to give lectures there. An invitation to hold a seminar on this subject in the University of the Witwatersrand provided me with an opportunity to remove some infelicities from the argument of the book. I should like to extend my thanks to the members of the staff of that University who made this possible.

For such inaccuracies as remain I am not only solely responsible but also truly sorry. They may put some readers in mind of one of my favourite quotations, which comes from the index to the first English edition of Grotius's *De Jure Belli ac Pacis* and reads as follows: "Historians, not to be trusted." I must hope that critics will be to some extent disarmed if I conclude with this quotation from Grotius's preface: "The same Liberty that I have herein taken, in judging of the Sentences and Writings of others, the very same, I say, do I heartily beg and intreat all, into whose hands this Book of mine shall come, to take in judging of me, and mine. They shall not be more ready to Admonish me . . . than I shall be . . . to follow their Advice."

F. H. HINSLEY

St. John's College
Cambridge
September, 1965

CONTENTS

vii

Nothing is today more greatly needed than clarity upon ancient notions. Sovereignty, liberty, authority, personality—these are the words of which we want alike the history and the definition; or rather, we want the history because its substance is in fact the definition.

HAROLD J. LASKI, *The Foundations of Sovereignty and Other Essays* (1921), p. 314

SOVEREIGNTY, SOCIETY AND THE STATE

M EN do not wield or submit to sovereignty. They wield or submit to authority or power. Authority and power are facts as old and ubiquitous as society itself; but they have not everywhere and at all times enjoyed the support or suffered the restraints which sovereignty, a theory or assumption about political power, seeks to construct for them. Although we talk of it loosely as something concrete which may be lost or acquired, eroded or increased, sovereignty is not a fact. It is a concept which men in certain circumstances have applied—a quality they have attributed or a claim they have counterposed —to the political power which they or other men were exercising.

What has been the function of this concept? What has distinguished it from other ways of thinking about political power? Whatever men may feel about it in advanced societies —even if in such societies it has sometimes been used to convey different meanings—the term sovereignty originally and for a long time expressed the idea that there is a final and absolute authority in the political community. This idea may have been expressed more or less emphatically. For some men it may have seemed necessary, for example, for others otiose, to add the thought that no final and absolute authority exists else-where than in the community. In truth such glosses add nothing essential to the notion. If we wish to explain why men have thought of power in terms of sovereignty we have but to explain why they have assumed that there was a final and absolute authority in their society—and why they have not always done so.

What are the circumstances, then, in which they have resorted to this assumption? One clue to the answer to this further question is the absence of any notion of sovereignty in the primitive stages of political societies. Another is the fact that, in the history of every society in which the issue of sovereignty has arisen, the issue has been more hotly debated at some stages than at others. Another is the tendency for men in sophisticated political societies to attenuate or deny this attribute of political power which the earlier history of political theory makes it impossible for them merely to ignore. All these clues lead in the same direction. The concept has been formulated when conditions have been emphasizing the interdependence between the political society and the more precise phenomenon of its government. It has been the source of greatest preoccupation and contention when conditions have been producing rapid changes in the scope of government or in the nature of society or in both. It has been resisted or reviled—it could not be overlooked—when conditions, by producing a close integration between society and government or else by producing a gap between society and government, have inclined men to assume that government and community are identical or else to insist that they ought to be. In a word, the origin and history of the concept of sovereignty are closely linked with the nature, the origin and the history of the state.

The Nature and Origin of the State and its Relationship to Society

In modern political societies men have often insisted that, like sovereignty, the state itself is only a concept, "a fiction of philosophers", "a myth". Even if we agree, however, that "there is no such thing as the power of the state, only the power of individuals",[1] it remains necessary to recognize that the state—or at least the instrument of power to which we should apply this term—exists in the phenomenal world. Properly used, the state is the name we attach to one among the various political institutions which societies develop. It is a distinctive political institution, the particular means of organizing political power which societies have adopted at a particular stage in their evolution.

In the past hundred years in advanced communities its growth has been so enormous, it has so overshadowed all other associations, that it has sometimes gone far towards absorbing all the functions of society. This has made it difficult for us to grasp that it is not the political society itself in some special form or at some particular stage of its development, so that state and society have become virtually interchangeable terms. But the political institutions of societies should not be confused with the societies themselves; and it should not be overlooked that the state is different in important respects from other political institutions. These two distinctions are central to an understanding of the history of political thought, not to speak of a proper understanding of history and politics.

To illustrate the first of them it is sufficient to make two points. At no time, in no society, has the political system been the only agency or institution in the community. In the most advanced societies, as in the most primitive, the law it lays down is never the sole code regulating social behaviour, and the role of citizen is but one of several roles which each man plays as a member of society. The power and competence of the political system has varied from society to society and from time to time in every society; the question of what should be its power and competence has always been debated.

<hr />

[1] M. FORTES and E. E. EVANS-PRITCHARD, *African Political Systems* (1958 edn.), introduction by A. R. Radcliffe-Brown, p. xxiii.

But at no time, in no society, has its identification with, or control over, the society been complete. Even under the régime of the state, the most powerful and effective of all the political institutions which societies have so far developed, and even under the rule of the most powerful of states, other institutions exist alongside it, men still speak of "we" and "they", and it is not uncommon for the society to limit the state by laying down fundamental rules by which it may or may not undertake certain tasks. And this situation, secondly, is a reflection of the fact that a society and its political system have different origins, a different relationship to functions.

A political society serves many functions; it does not come into existence to serve them. It serves the functions because it exists, but it exists because of the nature of men and because of the fact—and to the extent—that men live together. We know no more than this about its origins; but more than this we do not need to know. What is true of the society, is equally true of some of its components—of the family, for instance, or of the racial minority. It is only partly true, on the other hand, of a society's political institutions. In the sense that every society that is a political society possesses some political system there is no problem about the origins of political institutions. Since different societies develop different political institutions, however, and since the same society adopts different political institutions at different stages in its course, the problem of origins cannot be avoided. The anthropologist or the sociologist may properly conclude that the origins of the various political institutions of societies cannot be discovered, for these may be hidden in the mists of time. He should not say that there is no point in discovering them, for that is to confuse what we need not know with what we may not be able to learn.

Least of all should he say this of the origins of, among these political institutions, the state. For while all societies, however primitive, possess political institutions—while the possession of a political system is, indeed, an indispensable condition of being a society, so that "intermittent action by the oldest male ... or informally formulated consensus on the part of a group ... implies a special type of political structure, not its absence"[1]—we cannot say that every society must develop the state. Nor has every society as yet developed it. We inhabit a world in which there still exist both stateless political societies and societies which are ruled by states. The distinction between the state and other political institutions is as decisive as is the distinction between a society and its political system.

This last statement is not universally accepted because it is possible to consider political institutions from two different points of view. We may emphasize the common function which they all serve; or we may classify them by the different ways in which they serve that function. From the first point of view it is logical to say that, since every society has a political system and since the function of every political system is the maintenance of a social order within a territorial framework by the exercise of authority, then every form of government, every political system, is essentially a state at some stage in its evolution. By this definition it does not matter where the ultimate authority may rest, or how far it may be dispersed, or whether it is indeterminate or even discontinuous. The most primitive political system contains at least the rudiments, is at least a foreshadowing, of the state. Even the Australian aborigines whose various clans meet together from time to time in religious assemblies which have some power to regulate disputes between the groups, even the Bushmen bands in which the male elders exercise purely psychological and moral coercion, may be regarded as being a recognizable if impermanent government system and thus a recognizable if minimal version of the state. From the second point of view,

[1] Quoted in S. N. EISENSTADT, *The Political Systems of Empires* (1963), p. 6.

in contrast, it is not the similarity of function that is significant but the different ways in which the function of upholding order is performed or attempted. By this approach the state differs from other political institutions by the fact that it performs this standard function in a distinctive manner—not by its claim to or investment with the final power of coercion, for such a power may be recognized in societies which do not have the state, nor even by any greater effectiveness or continuity in wielding this power, though this may be its result, but by the fact that it exercises this power in a particular way.

Of these two points of view the first has this to be said for it. In the history of many societies the emergence of the forms of the state will have followed after stateless institutions and will often have built upon them; and in any attempt to classify societies at varying stages of growth we must thus expect to find them exhibiting the characteristics of varying stages in a slow historical transition from the stateless condition to the acceptance of the state. Using this approach it may seem difficult, indeed impossible, to say when the stateless condition has ended and the state has become established—to specify in an extended succession of changes of degree the point at which their accumulation constitutes a change of kind—and this makes it tempting to regard the transition to the state as a continuum of stages in which the state is foreshadowed from the outset. But it is necessary to distinguish between the historically slow process by which a stateless society comes to be subjected to the state and, on the other hand, the qualitative change that has been effected when that process is completed. If we make this distinction, and if we concentrate on the nature, the quality, of the transition instead of on the process in time by which it is accomplished, then there is little doubt that the institution of the state represents a change of kind. For there is ample evidence that even at the most primitive level of the state the differences are immense between those political communities which do, and those which do not, accept its rule. So much is this so that to argue that the stateless society and the society ruled by the state are essentially similar in respect of their political institutions is no more helpful in the field of political science than would be the statement in the field of the natural sciences that a man and a cockroach are essentially in the same family because they both have legs and need to eat.

The stateless society—this is the most obvious difference— has no single central symbol or instrument of rule, is acephalous and segmentary, whereas a single headship is the mark of the presence of the state. But it is not enough to point this out, for the actual power of the central rule, of the state, may in fact be minimal; the society in which it exists may remain segmentary in many other respects if not in this. It must be stressed that, however weak its actual power, the existence of the state still involves a fundamental change in the pattern of authority within the society in which it has come to exist. The various extant societies of Africa, for example, comprise some which are stateless societies and others which are ruled by primitive states. In the stateless societies the political system is based on lineage segments or on such tribal institutions as age-grades. Political activities and relationships are conducted through lineage or tribal relationships in lineage and tribal divisions even if these happen to be also territorial divisions. In the societies which are ruled by the primitive states, on the other hand, the framework of political activity is an administrative organization which regulates the relations between territorial segments, and these segments are also the administrative and judicial units. While kinship and lineage ties remain important they do not constitute the basic ties but rather cement the ties established by the administrative system. It is not too much to say that the administrative system

in these primitive states, unlike the lineage or tribal structure
in the stateless societies, "is never the kinship system writ large,
but is organized on totally different principles".[1]

This is reflected in the different political behaviours of the
two types of community. In and between the stateless communities, where the territorial segments cohere around local
lineages and the jural institutions rest on the right of self-help,
there is a balance of opposed local loyalties and ritual ties. The
resort to force as between the segments is usually tacitly
avoided, but if force is used against one segment by another
it is met only by equal force. The notion of defeat is normally
absent. The weaker of two segments will retreat rather than
fight, and if one segment does defeat another it does not
attempt to establish political dominance over it. In these
respects the pattern of conflict in and between these communities resembles that which operates in and between the
species of animals and birds. In the societies ruled by primitive
states, on the other hand, it is not merely the case that the
segments are defined in terms of administrative machinery and
that jural institutions rest on constituted judicial machinery.
The ultimate control of this machinery by the state is taken
for granted as the foundation of social order—and this despite
the fact that the delegation of power to regional chiefs is
practised on the ground that power should be dispersed and
rule be by consent, and not simply because of the physical
difficulty of administration from the centre. If a king evades
this constitutional limit to his power the subordinate chiefs are
liable to revolt; but in the event of rebellion the aim is to
change the ruler, not to abolish the rulership or to establish a
new form of government. If a subordinate chief becomes too
powerful the central authority is supported by other subordinate chiefs in the measures it takes against him. No less segmentary in some respects than the stateless society, so that reversion

[1] FORTES and EVANS-PRITCHARD, op. cit., p. 6.

to the stateless condition may be an ever-present possibility, the society ruled by the primitive state is in these respects the antithesis of the stateless society so long as it is so ruled. And the same is true of its external conduct, where the war for conquest and the stand against superior attack, behaviours which are uncharacteristic of stateless communities, are typical of the society ruled by the state.

These differences in the pattern of authority and of conduct go far to destroy the argument that every political system, however primitive, is a foreshadowing of the state—that all political systems should be classed as different versions of the state at different stages of its destined full development within every political society. They strongly suggest that, while stateless societies can attain to different degrees of organization, the natural ties of kinship reach a culmination in the lineage system of politics—which is a system of permanent unilateral descent groups in which corporate kinships acquire political functions—and the political capacity of stateless tribal relationships reaches a culmination in some such system as that of age-grades—which may unite a whole tribe in a way that lineage segments do not. They equally strongly suggest that the transition from the lineage or tribal system to the state, to the administrative system of political control, involves a leap or a shock which switches the political development of a society from its earlier, natural, stateless course and establishes in it the central authority and the administrative forms to which we give the name of the state.

This suggestion is not invalidated by the fact that most of the societies known to us have undergone this transition, or by the fact that all societies face the prospect of undergoing it: the leap or shock may be as natural as stateless development in the sense that it results from forces or contingencies which few societies are likely to escape for ever, if even for long. But when we turn to consider what those forces and contingencies may be—when we leave the qualitative difference between the stateless condition and the society ruled even by the primitive state for the complex problem of the historical origin of the state—we must not only notice that some societies have nevertheless not yet undergone the transition. There is this further consideration.

The fact that the leap or shock is one which it has been common for societies to experience stands in sharp contrast to the fact that historically the transition has been painful and slow, and one which societies have proved reluctant to undertake. And this contrast suggests that the first emergence of the state reflects not the desire of a society for its kind of rule but an urge in men to possess its kind of power. It is because this urge is so prevalent and perennial that, if this suggestion is right, the transition to the state has so commonly taken place. But the state has not everywhere emerged—and it has not succeeded in getting established wherever it has emerged—because the resistance of the society and the difficulty of the process of establishment are countervailing forces which may at any time in the early stages prove too strong.

Support for this argument is provided by the fact that in Africa, where we find stateless societies and primitive states side by side, there are no differences in general social conditions to explain the presence and the absence of state forms. In all the African systems which have been studied, in the primitive states no less than in the stateless societies, the economy is a subsistence economy in which distinctions of rank and status are partly independent of difference of wealth. In so far, moreover, as the economies differ while all being at subsistence level, these differences are not consistently aligned with the presence of the administrative political system. Where this—the state—exists, it exists regardless of whether the society is based on settled or on shifting agriculture:

indeed, while the Tallensi, with fixed agriculture, do not have it, the Bemba have it although they are shifting agriculturalists. As with type of economy, so with numbers. The society is larger numerically in the societies ruled by primitive states than it is in the stateless systems: the tribal and lineage systems may well be incapable of uniting for defence and the settlement of disputes as large a population as can the administrative system. Yet it does not follow that the tribal or lineage systems have given way to the state simply when numbers have passed a certain point. It is equally possible that a lineage or a tribal system divides if the population reaches a certain size without acquiring the state. And certainly there is no correlation between the presence of the state and the areas of highest density, as opposed to size, of population. Must we not conclude that, while roughly the same political function has to be performed in these various roughly similar societies, this function can be performed equally well by stateless systems as by the primitive state? Is not some additional feature required to explain the presence in such societies of the state which even in its primitive form carries out this standard function in a distinctive manner? And is it not likely that the explanation is to be found in the fact that it exists wherever circumstances have favoured and assisted the ambition to establish its power?

This conclusion is borne out by a closer study of those African societies where the primitive state is of comparatively recent origin, with a history of a hundred and fifty or two hundred years, and remains in its most primitive form. These societies—tribes which acknowledge a royal clan or chiefly line—exist alongside, and otherwise indistinguishable from, segmentary tribes where authority is associated with several aristocratic lineages or dominant clans or landowner lines and where it seems clear that kingdoms have often emerged without being able to prevent the tribes from relapsing into the segmentary condition in circumstances which make for a low survival rate for kingdoms. In those tribes which retain the forms of the primitive state the royal lineage is still only one of a number of similar lineages in the society, so that its position remains subject to challenge. In the royal lineage itself succession disputes are frequent, the number of royal relatives being large on account of the corporate nature of lineage and the practice of polygamy, and the difficulty of establishing such rules as primogeniture being immense for the same reasons. Because of the physical difficulties of communication the tendency is endemic, even in these small kingdoms, for royal princes to establish independent dynasties of their own in the provinces assigned to them by the central government. What characterizes the more stable among these states is the fact that, as in Buganda, they have surmounted these initial difficulties by their success in replacing clan heads in the provinces by administrative chiefs and in eliminating royal princes entirely from political positions; and what explains their success in these directions is often some fortuitous factor affecting the balance of power within the society such as access to an external supply of guns.

When the tendency to attempt the building of these primitive states is, despite these difficulties, so endemic—as endemic as the tendency of these societies to proliferate states by subdivision or to recede to the stateless condition—we cannot but conclude that although the state is an artefact the ambition which leads men to make it is both a natural urge and a central factor in the origin of the state. So much is this so that there is no necessity to embrace the conquest theory of the origin of the state. Given the close contiguity in most ages and many areas of the divergent social and cultural groupings into which men have been divided, and given this urge in men to establish the greater power that goes with the existence of state forms of rule, we ought not to be surprised if the emergence of the state has often been accompanied by the quest of some cultural groups for domination over others. No historian will doubt that the consolidation, if not the origin, of the state has often been assisted by conquest. It is not for nothing that the areas of the world in which we still find stateless societies are remote or inhospitable—Pacific Islands or African tracts. Nor should it pass without notice that, while most of the stateless societies of Africa consist of closely related linguistic and cultural groups, the societies in which primitive states have established themselves are mainly heterogeneous amalgamations of different peoples, each of which remains aware of its distinctiveness in origin and history. We might be tempted to deduce from this fact that the forms of the state have emerged only in the wake of and as a result of such amalgamation, and that such amalgamation has resulted only from conquest. But the most that can safely be deduced from it is that, while a stateless political system remains adequate for a community made up of closely related groups, there is need for the differently based and differently organized authority of the state if different groups are to be held together in a single political society. This would be true whether the amalgamation had resulted from conquest or in other ways; and true whether the amalgamation had preceded the state or the state had preceded the amalgamation. And from the little we know about the historical origins of the state, in Africa and in other areas, it seems plain that the amalgamation of different populations has followed upon the rise of the state in a homogeneous society as often as the establishment of state forms has followed upon the amalgamation, by conquest and in other ways, of culturally different groups.

In Africa the forms of the state have been established within homogeneous communities when a community without a chief has called in a chief from another society to rule over it; or when a community has developed administrative forms around (or in opposition to) raiders for slaves or booty; or when one of the noble lineages has been able to extend its power beyond that of the others on the basis of its access to guns.[1] In much the same way urban leaders in the Oman area have attempted in this century, under the influence of the discovery of oil, to bring resisting but homogeneous tribes into greater cohesion and greater dependence on an urban centre.[2] The Cherokee in North America, to take another example, similarly took the first step beyond the stateless condition—transformed themselves from an aggregation of independent villages into a tribal state—between 1730 and 1770, when neighbouring South Carolina threatened to cut off its supplying of ammunition if Cherokee attacks on its traders did not cease. They were forced to become a political community, with some administrative forms to control their own raiders, in order to avoid being left defenceless, without ammunition, against other Indian tribes.[3] It is equally clear, moreover, that political development towards the administrative forms of the state among homogeneous peoples can lead as effectively as the conquest of one group by another to the mixing of populations in an area. In the history of West Africa the rise of chiefs has encouraged trade and the mixing of peoples as often as the mixing of peoples has facilitated the establishment of chiefs.[4] In some African societies chiefs have strengthened their positions by attracting refugees and visitors from other societies into a protector-client relationship.[5]

It may be added, finally, that just as the royal authority in

---

[1] LUCY MAIR, *Primitive Government* (1962), pp. 109–22; JACK GOODY, "Feudalism in Africa", in *Journal of African History*, IV, No. 1 (1963), pp. 14–15.

[2] P. LIENHARDT, "Village Politics in Oman", in *Man* (1957), pp. 56–7.

[3] F. GEARING, "Priests and Warriors . . ., Cherokee Politics in the 18th Century" in *Memoirs of the American Anthropological Association* (1961–2), No. 93.

[4] GOODY, loc. cit.

[5] MAIR, op. cit., 112–15, 121–2.

African primitive states is sometimes based on the tradition of the first occupation of the land as against the influx of "strangers", and not on conquest, so the authority of the dominant clans in the stateless societies is associated with conquest as often as it is associated with this tradition.[1] To the conclusion that the amalgamation of heterogeneous elements in a single community may result from the rise of the state as easily as it may precede it, we may thus add this further conclusion. As the state has not always originated in the conquest of one cultural group by another, so such conquest has not always led to the establishment of the state.

The Relevance of the Relationship between Society and the State to the Concept of Sovereignty

If the desire to establish a degree of power and organization beyond the capacity of lineage and tribal forms is ubiquitous among men—and so much so that a variety of special circumstances and not conquest solely, among homogeneous no less than among heterogeneous groups of men, have equally been grist to its mill—it remains the case that the transition to the acceptance of the state has historically been a long and reversible process. It is accordingly reasonable to suppose that this desire, by whatever forces it is assisted, and even if those forces include the fact that the community may benefit from the establishment of the state, conflicts with the natural ways of undeveloped societies. The distinctiveness of the state—a distinctiveness which lies in the fact that, at least in its early days, it performs simple functions in a distinctive way—arises because the state imposes itself on its society, or attempts to do so, as the instrument of a power that is alien to those natural ways.

[1] AUDREY I. RICHARDS, "African Kings and their Royal Relatives", *Journal of the Royal Anthropological Society*, Vol. 91, Part 2 (1961).

In a stateless society authority relies on psychological and
moral coercion rather than on force; if it resorts to force it
does so because the rules and customs of the society demand
this. The moral coercion and the force, if force is used, may be
exercised by elders or other leaders but the structure of
command invariably emanates directly from the community.
It is the will of the community that it exerts, the custom of the
community that it upholds, and it is the structure of seniority
for non-political as well as for political purposes. The state,
on the other hand, is a structure of command imposed upon
the community in which it rules or attempts to rule. At its
earliest beginnings, it seems, it possessed this characteristic.
In the archaic societies of ancient Greece which Homer was
describing in the seventh century B.C.—societies which were
no longer stateless but in which the state was far from being
fully established—the rule of kings was already distinguished
from the power of other tribal leaders by being described as
rule "by might".[1] A king either had the might or did not rule.
His kingliness might be accepted as inborn and natural, but it
was justified by the fact that he was stronger, richer and more
splendid than anyone he ruled.[2] So long as it remains primitive
the state insists on this characteristic, so that in Buganda, for
example, on the principle that "a kingdom is always conquered,
not succeeded to", the Kabaka is enjoined at his accession to
"fight your enemies—conquer Buganda".[3] Whenever the
state has been successfully established we shall find that there
has been a struggle between the principle of community and
the principle of dominance, between the persistence of the old
methods and customs of a society and the claims of the kind
of government which only a power outside the society can

[1] M. I. FINLEY, *The World of Odysseus* (1956), pp. 22, 91–3, 116–17.

[2] F. E. ADCOCK, "Greek and Macedonian Kingship", in *Proceedings of the
British Academy* (1953), pp. 164–5.

[3] A. I. RICHARDS, in *The King's Men: Leadership and Status in Buganda on
the Eve of Independence* (ed. L. A. Fallers, 1964), p. 284.

provide, and that the state is the outcome, however marginal, of the victory, however delayed, of the latter.

It is in this way that the rise of state forms is a necessary condition of the notion of sovereignty, of the idea that there is a final and absolute political authority in the community. In a stateless society this idea is irrelevant. Even when it possesses a final authority that is fully effective for its purposes, such a community lacks the kind of government, separate from it and yet wielding the power which is essential to its continued existence, to which the idea can be applied. In the absence of the state, the basis and the use of this power cannot become the subject of conflict and debate; so that even though such a community is not free from political struggles, the issue in these struggles is not the basis and use of this power but whether disaffected elements or segments will hive off and establish a separate community. But when a society is ruled by means of the state the concept of sovereignty is sooner or later unavoidable. Questions about the final authority, what that implies and where it lies, must sooner or later in such conditions acquire a fundamental and perhaps a permanent significance.

It may nevertheless be later rather than sooner that the concept of sovereignty emerges in the wake of the rise of the state. The state can establish itself in a community without giving rise to this concept, even as a political community can exist without the state. In the history of societies, indeed, the appearance of the forms of the state has not usually been followed at once, if followed at all, by the discussion of political power in sovereignty terms. Nor is it possible to explain this delay by supposing that there has naturally been a time-lag between the appearance of the state and the beginning of any conscious analysis of the state's claims; for sovereignty has not been the first concept to emerge even when men have embarked on conscious analysis of its claims. If the state is a necessary condition of this concept, it is not a sufficient condition of it. What seems to have been further required before men have advanced this explanation of the basis of rule is that they have ceased, to a sufficient extent, to regard the state as alien to the society and have to some extent begun to identify the claims of the state with the needs of the community.

Another way of stating this point presents itself if we recall that the community may remain segmentary in many respects even after the forms of the state have appeared, and even after they have been accepted, within it. Indeed this phase in the development of the relations between a community and its state has been experienced so widely as to justify the use of the term "segmentary state" to connote the intermediate political system in which the administrative forms of the central state and the segmentary organization of power in the society are found in combination.[1] It has been so widespread in the history of societies that we shall not be far wrong if we suppose that it has been a normal if not even a necessary stage in the development of the state. Certainly it has not been evaded even by states which have been established in recent times and in developed communities—by states like the United States of America in the eighteenth century or the German Empire in the nineteenth century. But in considering the relation between the "segmentary state" and the notion of sovereignty these modern examples may still be misleading. Founded when they were, when that notion already had a long history elsewhere, they were segmentary states in which the concept of sovereignty was nevertheless central to the political attitudes of their rulers. The fact that they were formally established as federal states may, indeed, have been a necessary and logical consequence of this contradiction—the federal constitution being in large measure the formal compromise which is adopted when the concept of sovereignty exists in the segmentary political

[1] A. W. SOUTHALL, *Alur Society* (1956), pp. 238–60.

conditions which are strictly incompatible with it. If we ignore these modern examples we notice two things about the development of political thought during the "segmentary state" stage. Political theories have evolved *pari passu* with the development and extension of the state's administrative institutions as against traditional habits and customs. But ratiocination has still stopped short of the notion of sovereignty so long as the "segmentary state" has persisted—or at least for as long as the balance between the state and the segments, between the centre and the other wielders of power over whom the centre exercises only limited control, has not tilted so much to the centre as to enable men to attempt to replace the segmentary by the unitary state and the several hierarchical segments by a single hierarchical society.

The process by which this balance has shifted has commonly in history been as lengthy and as tortuous as that which has culminated in the first emergence of state forms. It has been no less reversible, so that societies ruled by segmentary states have reverted to a higher degree of segmentation under the state or to complete fragmentation under separate states as often as they have proceeded to the achievement of the unitary state. But there has been this difference between the two processes. The first emergence of the forms and institutions of the state seems often to have been the outcome of the power of men and their wish to rule, aided by accident and circumstances but owing little to the needs or the collaboration of the community. The further expansion and development of those forms and institutions, on the other hand, all that increase in the continuity, the professionalization and the scope of government which has been required before the balance could shift to the centre and the segmentary state could give way to the unitary state—these things have depended not only on the ambition and the power of rulers but also on the changes in the character of the community itself.

These changes may have been accelerated by the work of government. They may, alternatively, have owed nothing to that work, but have resulted from impersonal trends which were moving the society away from static conditions, a closed economy and the dominance of ascriptive groups towards differentiation in social, economic and political conditions. But rarely, if ever, have they been brought about solely by the efforts of rulers; and history abounds with examples of rulers who, as in the Mongolian and the Carolingian Empires, have made strenuous attempts to develop and professionalize the forms and institutions of the state, and to impose them on their societies, but who have failed for lack of the necessary momentum in their societies.

When both of these sources of change have been at work, as has often been the case, they have not merely co-existed. There has occurred a positive interpenetration of influence between the changing community and the expanding state machine. Yet a closer study of this process as it has taken place in the history of societies serves to emphasize another finding. While the process of interaction has become impelling and all-pervasive, dynamic and incessant, after a certain point in the development of some societies, that turning-point has ever been long delayed. The resistance of the customary society to the ways of the state, the disregard by the traditional ruler of the influence of the changing community, the persistence on both sides of the outlooks of the "segmentary state"—these are the impressive features, even after the introduction of the forms of the state, even in the development of the societies of Europe. Anyone possessing a nodding acquaintance with the histories of other societies—of ancient Egypt, for example, or the Chinese Empire or the Ottoman Turks—will recognize at least one general difference between them on the one hand and Europe on the other. In their histories this resistance was even more tenacious, this disregard even more complete, the advance of the mutual impact of government and society even more halting and slow, the turning-point even longer delayed—if it was ever achieved.

This seems to be the reason why even in the history of European societies the concept of sovereignty followed so long after the emergence of the state, and why—except by importation from Europe—it has not yet figured at all in the history of non-European societies. To understand the origin of this concept it is necessary to distinguish between the emergence of the state as a distinctive institution and, on the other hand, the extent to which the state is recognized and the extent to which its rule is effective. A community cannot be conscious of the state until its forms and its outlook have appeared; but the state cannot rule effectively until these forms and this outlook are not only recognized but also welcomed by the community in some degree—and have been modified by the community to some extent. It is when a sufficient element in the community in which the state operates has sufficiently come to accept it and when, in the process of becoming accepted to this sufficient extent, the state has adjusted its forms and its outlook to the demands and conditions of the community—it is then and only then, at the point when the state is ceasing to be a segmentary state, that the concept of sovereignty has been newly coined.

It is in this sense that, while the emergence of the state as a form of rule is a necessary condition of the concept of sovereignty, it is not a sufficient condition of it. A community and its government must be sufficiently distinct, as they are only when the government is in the form of the state, before the concept of sovereignty is relevant. But the appearance of the concept is still delayed until the community and its government, society and state, remaining necessarily distinct in some respects, have been integrated to a certain extent in others. It is only when the community responds to the state and the state responds to the community in which it rules that the discussion of political power can take place in terms of sovereignty.

The Definition and the Function of the Concept of Sovereignty

Four things should follow if the previous argument is tolerably accurate. The concept of sovereignty will not be found in societies in which there is no state. Far from arising at once with the emergence in a community of the forms of the state the concept will not have appeared until a subsequent process of integration or reconciliation has taken place between a state and its community. It will infallibly have struggled to the surface, on the other hand, whenever and wherever that process has advanced to a certain point. And then, once the concept has emerged in any society, its further development will have been ultimately linked with further changes in the relations between the society and its government. We must now turn to the history of political theory to discover whether these expectations are fulfilled.

This would be an easier task if it were not for the fact that the history of this concept, as of any similar idea, is full of pitfalls. Since this is so—since historians still debate, for example, whether the notion existed in classical Greece or in Western Europe in the thirteenth century—there must be some preliminary clearing of the ground. We must wrestle with the semantic problem which always arises in this kind of study. We are faced with another initial difficulty, equally complex—with the problem of the relationship of precise concepts to more general, or to inchoate, ideas.

The semantic problem derives from the fact that the terms and expressions of one age or civilization can sometimes be given only approximate equivalents when they are translated into the language of another. It is aggravated by our tendency to assume that, when ancient terms are still in use, the actual phenomena which once underlay them have undergone no change. Examples abound of the confusion that results when this tendency joins forces with translation difficulties. The fact that Aristotle used words which we must translate as "the state" or "the law" can lead us to believe that he meant what we mean by those words. We can easily forget that what the word "empire" conveyed to Charles V, or the word "federalism" to Kant, was something different from what it conveys to us. Nor is it only in our day that these difficulties have existed; they have affected political language and ideas at all times. And this has combined with another fact—with the powerful grip of previous example and achievement on later aspirations—to create one more danger for the historian of ideas. For a long time after the fall of Rome, because of the deep impression its long existence had made upon them, some men in Western Europe wrote and acted as if the Roman Empire still existed, as if its administrative and political forms were still in being, when the actual conditions of society were incompatible with the existence of so advanced a form of the state. Where the idea of sovereignty is concerned we may sometimes find that men did not possess it when a loose translation of their language persuades us that they did. But they might sometimes have inherited language properly associated with the idea without knowing the conditions that are necessary if the idea itself is to be viable.

This consideration might suggest a further question. Is it any less difficult to establish the truth about historical facts and conditions than it is to establish the truth about the history of ideas? How can we be sure that no such advanced form of state as the Roman Empire existed in the early Middle Ages? This is a relevant question. If we cannot be certain whether and to what extent the forms of the state have themselves existed at any particular time we cannot hope to establish that the forms of the state are a necessary condition of the concept of sovereignty or that their emergence has, even so, not usually been followed at once by the discussion of political power in terms of that concept. There is an essential difference, nevertheless, between the difficulties raised by this question and those in which the linguistic problem is involved. Whatever the pitfalls may be when we are seeking to discover whether state forms existed, and to what extent, in any particular society, however great our uncertainties in returning an answer, there is at least an objective test that can be applied to the evidence. When we ask whether and what men thought of those forms at any particular time, while we can again apply objective tests to distinguish the ways in which men have thought, we must first make sure if we can that they thought as we think they did.

The semantic problem constitutes part of this initial barrier. The other problem involved might be described as the opposite hazard. If there is a danger of misinterpreting and misunderstanding the ideas to which men have given expression in earlier times there is also the possibility that they entertained ideas to which they could not or did not give expression. With political ideas like sovereignty—or, to take another example, representation—this possibility is very real.

Other ideas, closely related to the notion of sovereignty and at least as central to political thought, have been expressed by men in most ages in the words for "power" and "rule", "empire" and "country", "king" and "government"; but they are less precise and specific, less technical and sophisticated, than is the idea of sovereignty. It is easy to conceive of situations in which men had some understanding of this more technical concept without having a specific word for it—in which perforce they used no word for it at all or else fell back on the words they used for less precise ideas like rule or empire or power. If it is right to envisage the emergence of the notion of sovereignty as a process reflecting the slow advance of mutual adjustment between a society and its state, we must expect, indeed, to meet such situations—to find Henry VIII of England using the word "empire" to express what we mean by sovereignty; to find that with this notion as with so many others there is a long preparation or prehistory as well as a long historical development after its first formulation.

All the more is this the case because of the nature of its association with the more general ideas of power and rule. As every political society possesses some political institution, however primitive, so every system of rule, however undeveloped, rests on some method of legitimation of the ruler and some pattern of accountability which the ruler observes. For it is in this way that rule has ever distinguished itself from mere political power. Sovereignty is a concept by which men have sought to buttress older forms of legitimation and accountability or on which they have hoped to base new versions of these means by which power is converted into authority. Its function in the history of politics has been either to strengthen the claims of power or to strengthen the ways by which political power may be called to account. It has been first summoned into existence at a stage in the history of societies when changes in the relationship between the community and the system of rule have made existing claims and existing checks inadequate or out of date. However delayed in the history of any society that stage may have been, sovereignty at its first inception has still been only a new solution of an existing problem, a new way of thinking about power and rule; and however novel this solution may have been when first formulated, it has still been only a development out of earlier solutions of that problem.

In what, then, does its novelty, if any, consist? If only in view of the nature of these other preliminary difficulties it would be fruitless to embark on a history of the concept before taking further the initial question of definition. In one sense the answer to it has already been given: at the beginning, at any rate, the idea of sovereignty was the idea that there is a final and absolute political authority in the political community; and everything that needs to be added to complete the definition is added if this statement is continued in the following words: *"and no final and absolute authority exists elsewhere"*. But if we are to appreciate the significance of the idea we must also add this thought. With the notion of sovereignty a new or at least an altered meaning has been acquired by every element in this statement—by "political authority", by "political community", by "final and absolute". It is when and because these terms are acquiring a new significance, indeed, that the notion of sovereignty itself is finally arrived at. If the concept of sovereignty is only a restatement of the permanent problem of deciding the basis of government and obligation within a political community, it is also nothing more—but it is nothing less—than the restatement of that problem which is made when the political community and its government are judged to be necessary to each other and sufficient unto themselves, and which will be retained for so long as they are so judged.

II

THE CONCEPT OF SOVEREIGNTY IN
THE ANCIENT WORLD

USING this definition, forewarned of the difficulties, how shall we answer the first question that arises in any attempt to survey the history of the sovereignty concept? Men will often in history have debated and quarrelled about who should rule, and by what right, without having reached this notion. When and where, in the long record of these debates and quarrels, did it first appear?

The Polis and the Ancient Empires

It is often held that the classical Greeks had developed the idea at least by the time of Aristotle, and that they were the first to grasp it. Certainly in the records of earlier civilizations —of ancient Egypt, for example, or of monarchical pre-classical Greece—we shall search for it in vain. But not even Aristotle's language about government bears out the view that he succeeded in formulating it. He classified the governments of the Greek city states, in accordance with the numbers of those in whom the ruling power was visibly placed, into monarchy, aristocracy and polity (the rule of the many); and according to whether the rulers governed in their own or the public interest, he further distinguished between tyranny and monarchy, between oligarchy and aristocracy, and between democracy and polity. It was on such quantitative and moral differences between types of power that he placed the emphasis, and not on some special quality like sovereignty which all or some types of rule might be said to claim or to possess. And it seems reasonable to suppose that this was not merely because he lacked a word with which to express such a quality. The evidence suggests, indeed, that there were two insuperable obstacles to the idea of sovereignty in his way of thought and in the political and social conditions which his thought reflected.

Writing in the fourth century B.C., at the end of a long development that had culminated in the previous century in the civilization of the classical city state, he was able to feel that "man is by nature a *polis*-being" and to conclude that the political society of the *polis* was the highest form of human association or community. He made no distinction, however, between the community and the state; his word *polis* which we translate as state did not distinguish between the two. And this reflected an actual situation in which the *polis*, while it had become a highly organized community, was still essentially a community where the outlook of its members had not yet freed itself from kinship and tribal limits, and where the structure of government had not yet sufficiently separated itself from the ways and institutions of the tribal society to produce the forms and procedures of the state. Just as Aristotle's thought was based upon distinctions between types of rulership, so political activity in the city states was dominated in his day by the question of which element should rule, for rule in those integrated communities carried comprehensive power; but it was not yet concerned with divisions of opinion about the policies of government or the basis of government authority, for the organs of a government authority that was separate from the tribal community had not yet developed. It was for this reason that the dividing line was so narrow between politics and sedition and that civil war was so endemic. It is in the same direction that we should look for the explanation of that other characteristic of the Greek city states which gave a special quality to their inter-city war—of the relationship between them and the total jural and ritual community of all the Greeks. If the city still lacked distinctive government institutions even after it had become a highly organized community, this was not only because it remained largely tribal in its domestic arrangements. It was also because each city formed part of this wider single but segmentary society which, though stateless itself, was sufficiently pervasive to constitute a further obstacle to the full development of the forms of the state in the separate city.

The second obstacle to the notion of sovereignty in these circumstances arose from these same characteristics of the *polis*. The *polis*, highly organized but lacking separate state forms, was instinctively anti-monarchical, its political battles revolving around the conflict between the aristocratic and democratic forms of republican rule. By classical times the cities had either discarded the earlier forms of kingship or had greatly limited the powers of the king as in Sparta, where the power of ephorate (magistrates) and the strength of the community structure had produced two kings instead of one and reduced each king to something like Aristotle's description of them as hereditary generals for life. We might therefore suppose that sovereignty in the *polis* was thought to lie in the body of its aristocratic leaders or the totality of its citizens. But as well as being a community without the separate forms of the state, the *polis* was conceived of as a community that was rightly ruled by the law and not by men—or at least by men who were bound by the law—and the Greek idea of the law was one that set a limit to the self-sufficiency of the community. The institutions and codes of the community could be changed by deliberation and legislation, though the most frequent device was to call in a single lawgiver to give a new code of law after a period of change or stress. Men thus understood the difference between man-made laws and the law. But after giving the laws the lawgiver could only retain power by becoming a tyrant; and this was not only because of the prevailing opposition to monarchy, but also because his laws themselves, embodying the dictates of the gods or of universal reason and thus conforming to the law, remained superior to the community and detrimental to the development of a separate rulership within it. There was no modern conception of law as positive lawmaking without restraint. The political community was the highest form of *human* association; but it was still subject to the law enshrining the rational principle which the gods handed down to men. It was not for nothing that Aristotle came closest to the notion of sovereignty when he suggested that it was better that superiority should be vested in this law that was above the community, rather than in any person or body of persons within the community.

However we account for this situation—were these characteristics of the Greek city state due to the fact that it remained physically a small community, the largest never exceeding the size of an average English county; or was it that the city remained physically small because of these characteristics?—it meant that the political society of which Aristotle was writing had not undergone that separation of the state out of the community which constitutes the necessary condition of the concept of sovereignty. When we turn to other political systems that were roughly contemporaneous with Aristotle— to the Kingdom of Macedon which had not experienced development towards the *polis*; to the Empire of the Achaemenids and their successor in Persia; to the Empire of Alexander the Great, the ruler of Macedon who succeeded the Persian ruler Darius, on his death in 330 B.C., as the King of Asia—we can see that they had at least undergone this internal process. But it is equally clear that, if the Greek city states remained communities without distinctive state forms, these kingdoms and empires, while they had evolved the forms of the state, remained states in search of communities.

So markedly had their state forms of government become distinct from the communities of the area in which they had arisen that the rulers did not—indeed, could not—consider these communities as the object or the area of their rule. On the one hand, like the rulers of ancient Egypt and the ancient Middle East before them, like the later Inca and Aztec emperors of the fourteenth and fifteenth centuries A.D., and not entirely unlike the Habsburg Holy Roman Emperors in Europe up to an even later date, they thought of themselves as lords of many communities and varied peoples, as kings of kings, as rulers of a whole continent if not of all the world. On the other hand, the impact of their forms of government upon the communities under their rule was negligible. Beneath the imperial superstructure, well geared though that might be to conquest and expansion, and beneath the sub-kings of these various provinces or countries, the reality in all the communities of the Persian Empire and of Alexander's Empire, as in the Macedonian society from which Alexander expanded, remained rule through and by the clan, the lineage organization which functioned between the smaller family and the larger tribal nation. The situation in the area of later Aztec and Inca rule was not dissimilar. If there was any movement within these communities towards the replacement of kinship by administrative forms, let alone towards the integration of government and society, it had not proceeded far when these empires collapsed.

This gap between the rulership and the communities beneath it, a central feature of these early empires if not of all imperial rule, was reflected in their attitude to government. They upheld a personal, absolutist and theocratic conception of rule in which the ruler was identified with the gods and the law. Unlike some older oriental kings and unlike the Pharaohs, the Persian ruler was not the partner, priest or vice-regent of the gods; but it was by the grace of the gods that he ruled. With their successor there was a reversion to complete theocracy. Alexander the Great died in 323 B.C. a god on earth, the son of Zeus as well as ruler of Macedon, Greece, Asia and Egypt. And unless we are content to use the term unpardonably loosely we can say that this outlook was incompatible with any conception of sovereignty. Sovereignty, properly defined, is a notion that can arise only when rule is both more comprehensive, in the sense that it governs a society, and more restricted, in the sense that it is anchored to a society, than was the extensive but superficial absolute rule which these empires wielded. By evolving distinct state forms of government they had crossed the first barrier to the emergence of this notion. But they had made little or no progress towards the further stage in which alone the notion can develop—the stage in which the forms of the state have extended their power within the community and become reintegrated to some extent with it.

The Hellenistic Monarchies

It was under the Hellenistic monarchs of the third century B.C. that the first steps were taken towards this further stage. In each of the three Hellenistic monarchies that arose out of half a century of warfare between the generals of Alexander the Great—the Kingdom of the Ptolemies in Egypt, that of the Seleucids in Syria and Mesopotamia, and that which was formed out of Macedon and mainland Greece—the most prominent developments were the territorialization of imperial rule and the beginnings of an association between the government and the community throughout the large, highly organized areas of power which resulted from this territorialization.

Although they were first and foremost rulers by conquest,

the Hellenistic monarchs embraced the idea of fixed territorial possessions, which was originally as foreign to them as to their predecessors, in the process of their mutual rivalry and conflict. In all three kingdoms, and especially in Ptolemaic Egypt, they then proceeded to organize their government and exploit their communities with a rigour unknown before this time, establishing primogeniture as the rule for royal succession and developing an elaborate bureaucracy and a vast army with which they controlled the economy, allocated the land, collected the taxes—governed. They began by staffing these administrative structures mainly from the Greek ruling classes, which at first remained largely separate from the natives who retained their own speech and writing. But in the course of time the organization and exploitation of the kingdoms produced its impact on the populations. The Greeks blended with the native masses; these latter played an increasing role in the administration and the army. Nor was it only in this way that the kingship became less divorced from the people, on account of the needs of organized government. The absolutist character of rule was also forced to compromise with Greek ideas and the concepts of the Greek city. If the Hellenistic city, ceasing to be a city state, became an island of stunted self-government in a sea of wider rule, or even a rung in the system of central administration and government, it retained a considerable local autonomy, while the Greeks who formed the ruling class under the monarchs—as residents in Greece, as conquerors and migrants in the other areas—retained some of the traditions of the *polis* and of Greek thought. And if the kingship was having its impact on the total community, this fact in its turn enabled the community to mould the outlook of the ruler, the Stoic doctrine of attention to duty and indifference to social position being particularly influential as it was expanded into a doctrine of vocation for the ruler.

The gap between community and state was thus somewhat

narrowed. But it was far from being closed by the time these kingdoms began to weaken at the end of the third century B.C. In Ptolemaic Egypt the incorporation of the local population into the army and the administration provided the opportunity for mutiny and revolt as often as it sought security against these developments; while the progress of the forms and attitudes of the kingship was not sufficient to guard against the succession of tyrannical or indolent rulers, palace intrigues and interludes of praetorian rule. The Seleucid kingdom, a vast area of diverse populations in which the central government was never more than temporarily successful in imposing its rule upon ancient cities and resentful tribes, was also constantly at war with eastern neighbours and, in the west, with the rising power of Rome. The Macedonian monarchy preserved its traditional power in Macedon itself, but it yielded but little of its absolutist character there, while in the rest of Greece its rule over the cities remained limited and insecure.

When these facts are borne in mind, when the contrast is considered between the new outlook in these monarchies and the limited extent to which they were able to put it into effect, it comes as no surprise to find that, while the concept of sovereignty still found no place in Hellenistic political thought, there was now some progress towards its formulation. Emperor-worship, the cult of the ruler or the dynasty, was the characteristic Hellenistic theory of rule. An ancient concept already in this area because "divinity was cheap"[1] in ancient times, emperor-worship had been revived in the days of Alexander the Great and was perpetuated by the Hellenistic monarchs. In Egypt, for example, where the kingship of the Ptolemies was no more than a change of masters to the inhabitants, the new rulers, taking care to conciliate and control the great temples and priesthoods which had come down from the Pharoah's days, were in return admitted to the

[1] A. L. BASHAM, *The Wonder that was India*, p. 86.

company of the national gods. But in addition the cult that legitimized or at least strengthened their rule in the eyes of their Greek subjects was the cult of Alexander as one of the gods and as their predecessor; and all the more was this the case because ruler-cult was now voluntarily embraced by the Greeks, to whom it had been an alien concept, and made an integral part of the polytheism of the cities. In the Seleucid and Macedonian kingdoms the rulers claimed from the outset for similar reasons to be descended from gods. At first sight this would seem to have been a development inimical to all movement towards the emergence of the concept of sovereignty; for ruler-worship emphasizes the divorce between government and community whereas the integration of government and community is a pre-condition of this other notion. On the one hand, however, we must not exaggerate the significance that was attached to ruler-worship either by the rulers, who were kings in fact before they were kings in name and who relied on their administration and their actual power far more than on this doctrine, or by their subjects. For these—at least for the Greeks—it did not normally involve the belief that the kings were divine, not men. And on the other hand there can be no mistaking the importance of the cult of the ruler, in the formal character in which it prevailed, in another direction.

In combination with the older Greek idea of the law as something of greater validity than the expressed wish of the community or the ruler, it helped to bring about the more novel dogma that seems to have had its origin in the Hellenistic period—the dogma that the king was "personified law". He was indeed placed above the community by being regarded as of the company of the gods; but this now made it possible to regard him as being equated with, as being the source of, the law that was above the community. In this respect Hellenistic theory went beyond the divinity of the ruler as it had been understood in the more ancient Near East and as it continued to be understood in contemporary ancient India. There, despite a similar move towards the territorialization of rule and the development of administration, the ruler, though divine in the earlier and the looser sense of being divinely appointed and governing by the grace of the gods, remained no less subordinate than the ruled to the divinely and externally ordained social order, to *dharma*. The Hellenistic identification of the ruler with the law was, in comparison with this situation, an important step towards the later development of the concept of the body politic—whose own law transcended any external dictates—and also towards the later emergence of the concept of sovereignty—which would insist that since the law was the law of the body politic there must be in the body politic some power that was supreme and thus above the law.

The Rise of the Concept of Sovereignty in the Roman Empire

The Hellenistic monarchies had advanced no farther than this beyond the thought of ancient India or ancient Egypt when they finally succumbed, at the end of the first century B.C., to the sway of Rome. By this latter date, however, at the time of the transition from the Roman Republic to the Roman Empire, the Mediterranean world was poised to take a further step towards that reintegration of the community and the state, towards that emergence of the idea of the body politic, of which the foundation had been laid under the Hellenistic kings. Until this time, although Rome was to be the only one of the thousand cities of classical Greece and Italy to succeed in dominating all the others, it was as a city community—a *polis*—that she had slowly and painfully built an empire since the eighth century B.C. Although, moreover, her process of empire-building would one day kill the *polis* as a political unit, much as the advance of the Hellenistic monarchies had tended to do, the ease with which she overcame those monarchies was due in part to her mobilization against them of the *polis* and the Greek tradition of republicanism in the name of freedom from royal autocracy. In addition, this process of conquest served only to consolidate the strength of city loyalty and the forms of the city community in Rome itself. It was to Rome as a city-kingdom that the Hellenistic world transferred the compliments of ruler-cult, regarding Rome itself as a goddess. And in reverse it was not a monarchy that evolved in Rome with the expansion of Roman rule, nor even any other form of rule that we can properly call a state, but the notion of "the Roman people's Empire" (*imperium populi Romani*)—a notion which, elaborated during the second century B.C., represented the maximum extension of the *polis* idea.

If only for this reason the Romans under the Republic no more developed the notion of sovereignty than did the classical Greek city states. The *populus Romanus* was the authority in whose name the magistrates enforced law. But the law still meant primarily what it had meant for Aristotle—not the will of the Roman people so much as the higher morality which it was Rome's duty to uphold. *Imperium*, in the same way, did not yet denote a political and territorial community governed by Rome. It was a power to rule which was conferred by the Roman people on its highest officials, as the title *imperator* was a title given to its victorious generals; and this power and this title could be held by several people simultaneously. As they were conferred by the people, we might be tempted to assume that the people was conceived of as being sovereign. But just as the absence of any notion of the Empire as a territorial entity prevented men from thinking in this way in relation to Rome's power beyond the city, so within Rome there was still an obstacle to this way of thought: the continuing submergence of what we would call the state in the total community of Roman citizens, into which the leaders of conquered communities were admitted.

If this is indicated by the evidence of the time it is confirmed by what took place after the end of the first century B.C., when party—or rather tribal—struggles within this community brought about the final collapse of the republican system. The replacement of the Republic by the Principate was a prominent step in the process by which state forms of rule were separating themselves out of the community and beginning to displace those of the city. It was followed by a period of transition of the kind which many societies have experienced during their passage towards acceptance of rule by the state— by a period in which the older tribal and ritual institutions of the city existed uneasily alongside the newer state forms. We may note in particular the persistence throughout the first century A.D. of the double rulership of the old and the new— of the Consuls, the Senate and the republican magistracies on the one hand and, on the other, of the Emperor who began in the constitution of 27 B.C. as merely the first citizen (*princeps civitatis*). It is equally clear that in this period, while it witnessed the steady consolidation of the Emperor's power and of the accompanying state system of rule, there was still no conception of the Emperor's sovereignty—as opposed to the early recognition of his personal superiority (*auctoritas*) over other authorities, of his personal absolutism and even, on some levels, of his divinity. But it was as a result of the nature of the transition—because the Emperorship was evolving out of the community forms which it slowly replaced, instead of being imposed upon them by conquest—that the Romans subsequently passed beyond the thought of the Hellenistic monarchies and arrived at the sovereignty notion.

Despite his original avoidance of the title of king or dictator, the Emperor possessed at the outset republican magistracies which made him the chief power in the state, and especially the *tribunicia potestas* which, according to Tacitus, the first Emperor devised so that "he might yet have some appellation by which he would overtop all the other authorities".[1] This was the basis of the *auctoritas* which made him superior to other magistrates with whom he still shared *potestas*. From the outset, by combining it with other ancient offices, especially the pro-consular *imperium*, he was continually extending it into a system of actual supreme rule in Rome; and he was exerting that rule over an increasingly unified territorial structure—a structure made up to his own special provinces; of the provinces which had originally been left to the Senate in conformity with the need or the desire to preserve the old organs alongside the new; of Italy; of Rome itself. The process amounted to the development of a new type of rule, rule by a single central authority, as is indicated by Tacitus's further remark on one of the first acts of Tiberius —his transferring of the election of magistrates from popular assemblies to the Senate which he had already subdued. "For though the Emperor already conducted the most important matters at his pleasure, yet till that day some were still transacted according to the inclination of the tribes".[2]

It was not for nothing, then, that the Emperor's *auctoritas* gradually became a formality. His rule came increasingly to rest not on this vague attribute but on the concrete reality of his pro-consular *imperium*, and this changed its significance, becoming exclusive to the Emperor and descriptive of his unique position. The title of *imperator* was quickly reserved by the Emperors for themselves—the old practice of granting it to successful generals was followed for the last time by the second Emperor, Tiberius; with Nero this hitherto honorary *praenomen* became the regular *praenomen* of the *princeps*. The original *imperium proconsulare* of the *princeps*, which had nominally been conferred by the Senate and which had distinguished him from other magistrates only by being soon extended for life and applied to several provinces, was shortly

[1] *Annals*, III, 56.   [2] ibid., I, 15.

after Vespasian's accession in 69 A.D. being generally confined to the Emperor and being used to refer to his absolute power. By the beginning of the second century it was itself being replaced for this purpose by the term *imperium* alone, in the generalized sense of the supreme power which had once belonged to the Republic or the People and which was different now from the proconsular *imperium* conferred upon the Emperor by the Senate. It was at this time, it may be noticed, that the last known *lex populi* was passed, the agrarian law of 96–98 A.D.

Parallel with this development in the nature of the governing power there occurred a change in its relationship to the territories in which it ruled. Not all Tacitus's disapproval of what he called "the shadows of imperial elevation"[1] conceals the fact that the consolidation of the state system of rule was the outcome not only of imperial effort but also of public welcome—or the fact that he himself regarded it as necessary for the public good. His *Histories* and *Annals*, written about the beginning of the second century, are filled with scorn for the alacrity with which all sections of society had scrambled on to the imperial bandwaggon. But they are filled as well with evidence that the imperial system, even while it was becoming increasingly a separate and professional structure of rule, was acquiring a new degree of control over its territories. Nor did this process slacken in the next century. The older republican families were progressively replaced by new classes of men in the important offices; these offices were increasingly filled by candidates from the provinces, so that the Senate came to represent the whole of the Empire and not merely Roman and Italian families and tribes; the holders of these offices, even if they served as senators, were firmly attached to the imperial civil service; and the civil service, like the military, steadily extended its grip throughout. By soon after the

[1] *Annals*, XIV, 47.

beginning of the second century there was no longer any opposition to the Empire as such. It is uncertain how far the tendency to replace the old title of the Empire, *imperium populi Romani*, by the new names of *imperium Romanum* and *orbis Romanum*, was indicative of these changes. But there can be little doubt that the declaration by imperial edict in the year 212 that all free persons who lived in the Roman world were henceforth Roman citizens was a step which reflected not only the omnipotence of the Emperor but also the fact that the Empire was centrally governed as the *imperium populi Romani* had never been—and perhaps in ways which that older structure could never have conceived.

The power of the Emperor was by then so complete that we may well doubt whether it differed in any essential respect from that of the ancient Persian emperors or the more recent Hellenistic kings—and this is all the more the case because there was increasing insistence on the divinity of the Emperor from the beginning of the second century. But differ it did, if only in the way in which it was thought about in the circles in which it was discussed at all. The Hellenistic king, unlike earlier rulers in the Middle East, had been both a god and the source or personification of the law; but this law had still been extraneous to the society, the law which he handed down. In the Roman Empire, even when the early compromise with the traditions of the *polis* had ceased and even though the Emperor had come to be widely regarded as a superhuman benefactor, the central doctrine in relation to the Emperor's position was, on the contrary, that he was *above the law*; and by the law was now meant the codes, customs and constitution of the society itself. These are the essential elements in a theory of sovereignty and it was now, from about the end of the first century A.D., that they were first enunciated.

They had grown up on the basis of the exemption from specific enactments which the first Emperor had been granted

as a special privilege. Although terminology remained impre-
cise—despite the fiction that the *princeps* was operating the old
republican system and despite the tendency to avoid any
classification which might restrict his freedom to do so—it is
clear that, like the Emperor's *imperium*, this limited exemption
came to be generalized until the general principle that the
prince was above the law became the prerogative of his
general *imperium*. Ulpian could lay this down as judicial
doctrine early in the third century: *princeps legibus solutus est*.
From there it was but a short and—given the growth of the
central imperial government and the needs of the state—a
natural step to Ulpian's other principle: "what has pleased the
prince has the force of law" (*quod principi placuit legis habet
vigorem*). Already by the middle of the second century the
Emperor had acquired this position by which his will was one
of the sources of law, by which he had legislative power as
such. But if his freedom in relation to the law was by then as
complete as that of any earlier ruler, he had arrived at it in a
different way. He had ceased to be the agent and had become
the head of a body politic. But he remained the head of a body
politic—and of a pre-existing body politic within which his
position had evolved—and so the law from which he was
absolved and which he could make was the law of the body
politic. Ulpian also laid it down as judicial doctrine that the
imperium of the Emperor had absorbed the original *imperium
populi Romani*.

Nor need we doubt that conflict between the ancient rights
of the community and a doctrine of pure ruler-supremacy
had played a large part in constructing and preserving the
more sophisticated doctrine of the legal supremacy of the
state in the interests of the community on which the imperial
power had then come to rest; for this conflict continued long
after the end of the first century A.D. Even though opposition
to the Empire as such had ceased by then, Emperors could still

be opposed if they failed to conform to Roman traditions or to the Stoic precept that the ruler should govern for the benefit of the ruled. There was no development of a hereditary right to succeed to the imperial throne in spite of the Army's preference for dynastic succession. This was because the Senate tried to maintain the republican traditions by insisting that the Emperor should be elected—so that adoption of a successor during the lifetime of the Emperor was the only possible stable compromise. Men who asserted the absolute supremacy of the Emperor were answered by theorists who maintained that the greatness of Rome had originated in the civic virtues rather than in the more recently established imperial structure of government—who proclaimed the enduring validity of the *imperium* of the Roman People; insisted that the Senate, representing the People, was still the sole legitimate source of the Emperor's powers; met the doctrines which exalted his rulership with the argument that the laws of the community were above the Emperor even if this must be by decision of the Emperor himself. And even after the Empire had in practice become a despotic régime— in spite of its increasing reliance on military force and on the myth of divinity after the end of the second century A.D.—the notion that the Emperor was in this way a constitutional monarch, who had reached his position by constitutional means, still survived in the laws of the Emperors themselves.

Which is why much later on, some centuries after the idea of sovereignty had disappeared there and also some centuries before it was recovered, men in Western Europe could find in the *Corpus Juris*, Justinian's compilation of Roman law, the *lex regia* doctrine—a doctrine declaring that, although power had been transferred to the ruler, the power of the ruler had had its rightful origin in the will of the People. *Quod principi placuit legis habet vigorem; utpote cum lege regia quae de imperio eius lata est, populus ei et in eum omne suum imperium et potestatem conferat.*[1] "What has pleased the Prince has the force of law; inasmuch as by the *lex regia*, which is passed with reference to his *imperium*, the People transfers to him and into his hands all its own right and power."

[1] *Dig.*, 1, 4, 1, p. v. and *Inst.*, 1, 2, 6.

III

THE EMERGENCE OF THE MODERN
THEORY OF SOVEREIGNTY

The Decline and Fall of the Roman Concept

Rome transmitted the conception of sovereignty in the form of the Emperor's *imperium* over the Empire, as it transmitted so much else, to the Middle Ages—directly to the Emperor's direct successors in Byzantium, indirectly to men in Western Europe. But the fall of the Roman Empire was followed in these areas—as also in Islam, the third main division into which the unity of the Mediterranean world was now divided—by a serious decline from the standards of Roman central administration and the victory of a religion based on revelation. Each of these three divisions long remained a single community in some respects. But these two developments produced conditions in which it was difficult, if not impossible, for men in any of these areas to continue to think of political power throughout the area in terms of sovereignty. The first re-established or threatened to re-establish a multiplicity of political societies. The second, even while it helped to preserve each area as a single religious community despite the existence of separate societies within it, established or threatened to establish the rule of God above the rule by men—to restore the sway of a law that was not the body politic's law.

Of the three areas Byzantium alone escaped these consequences. The Emperors at Constantinople were able to preserve the notion of their sovereignty over a unified empire —a notion purged by now of most of the constitutional implications which had played so large a part in its original conception and early development—because they also inherited in unbroken continuity with Rome the law, the forms and agencies of secular rule over a single society. In terms of the scope of his powers the Emperor had become an autocrat before the collapse of the imperial structure in the West. His successors in the Eastern Empire were able to obtain the right of the Emperor to crown his successor during his own lifetime and even to assert from time to time a hereditary and family right to the throne. But at least in theory the title to the imperial throne remained elective throughout the history of Byzantium and the ultimate source of the Emperor's power continued to be the consent of the people. The Emperor was chosen by the Senate or the Army, exercising inherited delegated rights. The choice proclaimed by Army or Senate was ratified by the acclamation of the People before the chosen was crowned. And if the coronation was carried out by the Patriarch of Constantinople, which was not essential, the Patriarch acted as the representative not of the Church, but of the electors. Once crowned, it is true, there was no constitutional method by which the autocrat could be removed. There was a continual reminder of his constitutional origin, however, in the fact that the Empire preserved the Roman practice of exacting an oath from the Emperor to the electors and the People to the effect that he would govern justly. And on this basis there was also perpetuated the Roman willingness to transfer loyalty to the successful usurper—the character, in Mommsen's words, of being "an autocracy tempered by the legal right of revolution".

It is also true that, once crowned, the Emperor in the East became the associate of God as well as the elected ruler of the society. From the ninth century, moreover, the priestly side of office was emphasized by the addition to the coronation ceremony of his anointment by the Patriarch with consecrated oil. But the imperial system escaped degeneration into theocracy, the main consequence of the spread of revealed religion, by retaining not only the elective element of the Roman system but also the Roman tradition by which the Emperor was head of the Church. Just as the Emperor was the elective ruler before he became the vice-regent of God on earth, so the system solved the problem of church and state by subjecting the leading cleric to the leading official: the Emperor himself appointed the Patriarch of Constantinople. And while this helped to shore up his authority, Christianity itself strengthened his character as a temporal ruler by precluding his deification. Although the Byzantine Emperors sedulously cultivated the Emperor-worship tradition of the East, as well as what Christianity contributed to the notion of the sacredness of the ruler, they did not become divine. From the fifth century onwards the Emperor was *Imperator Dei Gratia* but he was never to become *Divus Imperator*.

It was on the basis of these elements in the pre-Christian Roman system that, during all the centuries which stretched from the transfer of the Roman Empire to Constantinople to the final disintegration of their power after the beginning of the thirteenth century, the Eastern Emperors were able to uphold the theory that they were sovereign rulers of all Byzantium. Great territories were removed from Byzantine rule by the advances of Islam, the Turks and the Slavs. With the decline of commerce and communications the actual intervention of the central government in its remaining provinces became intermittent, and its actual authority died quickly with the increase in distance from the centre. But if imperial rule at most times creaked, and at some times verged on collapse, it continued to be based on a bureaucracy. If the structure of government reverted to being that of a "segmentary state" in practice, it retained the outlook and the body of theory which it had inherited from the unitary state of Rome.

Thus even when granting out fiefs to hereditary holders—
a practice which became essential on a wide scale, especially
on the borders of the Empire—the government succeeded in
maintaining the direct subordination of every fief-holder to
itself and in thus avoiding the hierarchy of independent vassals
and subordinate sub-vassals which became characteristic of
European feudalism.

It was not for nothing, then, that as late as the fifteenth
century Byzantine scholars not only still scorned local or
provincial affiliations but also still gloried in the imperial
rather than the Christian name—calling themselves Byzan-
tines when they did not insist, as was still more common, on
calling themselves Romans.[1] We shall not be far wrong if we
think of Byzantium as having persisted as a single structure of
society ruled by a state which was in slow decline but which
was saved for centuries from disruption, though not from vast
losses of territory, by the resilience of the agencies and attitudes it had inherited from Rome—as also by the menace of
the advancing infidel and by its scorn for the despised barbarian in the West. When we turn, however, to the infidel
and the barbarian, to Islam and to Western Christendom, we
find that the outcome was different. They experienced a far
more serious decline than did Byzantium from the unity and
the administration which had prevailed under the rule of
Rome. In parallel with their political disorder, and perhaps in
consequence of it, they also experienced more extreme effects
from the impact of religion. So much was this so that the
problem which arises when we consider the over-all political
character of either of these areas during the Middle Ages is
not to decide how far it was a single society ruled by a single
unitary state. It is to decide whether it was a single political
society, held together by a single but highly segmentary state

[1] D. J. GEANAKOPLOS, *Greek Scholars in Venice* (Harvard, 1962), p. 205;
S. RUNCIMAN, *Byzantine Civilisation* (1933), p. 29.

only because it was also a single ritual community, or whether it was some looser structure still—not a single though segmentary society but a congeries of separate political communities to which religion gave a common but a non-political bond.

Medieval Islam soon developed the characteristics of the latter of these structures. Lacking any direct continuity with imperial Rome and being directly based on the conquests and conversions of a religion, its original central authority, the Caliphate, lost control of Spain and Western North Africa by the end of the eighth century; of Egypt, Crete and lands in Arabia and further east during the ninth century. Soon after the beginning of the tenth century—after an attempt to compensate for the loss of geographical empire by becoming in its remaining Persian lands not only the leader of the faithful but also the absolute monarch of its subjects after the fashion of the ancient Persian emperors—it was deprived of all its remaining strictly temporal power, was reduced to the position of a religious figurehead, by the rise of conquest empires in Persia itself. On the other hand—though only with the aid of the fiction that there could be only one Caliph, for separate Caliphates had by then been established in Spain and North Africa—Islam as a whole continued to be theoretically headed by a theocratic Caliph who did not actually rule.

Initially the Prophet had succeeded by preaching the superiority of the One God to differing tribal customs among Arabs who knew only one kind of ruler: the chief by consensus of a tribe or of an agglomeration of clans. In an area where society remained at this stage, the tribes and clans being little affected by the rise and fall of conquest emirates, the original doctrines of the Prophet lost none of their force. Islam was the community of Allah in which Allah alone was the mundane head, governing and making the laws, with the Prophet as

His agent and mouthpiece. After the death of the Prophet only the Caliph, as Mohammed's successor, could be the highest authority; his authority could know no distinction between the spiritual and the temporal spheres. Since, however, the death of the Prophet had destroyed the sole means of knowing Allah's further will and of changing Allah's laws, the Caliph's supreme power was confined to upholding the laws already set down in the Koran and in the Prophet's sayings—and to spreading the reign of these laws by the holy war. He had no capacity to change the laws or to add to them, nor was he in a strong position to develop such a capacity in relation to communities where most men insisted that he possessed his authority only if confirmed in office by the consensus of the faithful and where some even doubted whether any man but the Prophet himself could be the representative of God.

The resulting extreme but powerless theocracy underlay the central feature of Islamic theories of government. Faced with the problems of reconciling the position of the Caliph as necessarily the highest authority in a single ritual community with that of the many emirs and sultans who were the actual wielders of power, under the sway of a religion and a law which insisted on the unity of spiritual and temporal authority, the jurists added to the fiction that there could be only one Caliphate the further fiction that all actual political power was a delegation of his power in the temporal field by the Caliph. It was a theory which could be stretched very far —to establish the legality of any usurping sultan or conquering emir on the principle that all power was legal which conceded allegiance to the Caliph; to permit a sultan or an emir to designate a Caliph on the principle that he to whom the effective ruler conceded allegiance was the Caliph; to justify even the sultan or emir who deposed the Caliph or seized the Caliphate for himself, as did the Ottoman Turks in 1519 in their determination to end the dual system of rule, on the principle that the faithful could remove a Caliph if he acted contrary to the law and on the principle that the Sultan or the emir was acting for the faithful. But if only because it could be so stretched, to legitimize all actual power however established and to oblige the believer to obey whoever actually ruled, this structure of ideas was viable so long as Islam continued to be made up of basically tribal societies which were tenuously governed by absolutist conquest rulers, as was the accompanying distinction between higher government, based on revealed law, and positive government—government based on human reason which merely safeguarded men against disorder.

It was incompatible, on the other hand, as incompatible as were these actual conditions, with any development of the notion of sovereignty either over Islam as a whole and within its separate Caliphates or within the different political societies of which the Caliphates were composed. Within a Caliphate or within Islam as a whole, the actual rulers governed under the Caliph, as positive government operated under the sway of higher government; and the Caliph ruled for and under God. God was thus absolute in the Caliphal community, and neither the nature of His power nor the nature of that community, the community of all the faithful, was technically conceivable in sovereignty terms. Such a hierarchy of authority was similarly incompatible, as incompatible as were the actual conditions, with the development of the idea of sovereignty within any of the various societies of which Islam or any of the Caliphates was made up. While it was perfectly consistent with absolutist rule within the society, it made it unnecessary, perhaps impossible, for government to rest its claim to allegiance on the powers it exercised and the functions it performed within the society. As the actual conditions changed within some of these communities, as the links between governments and societies developed, from about the beginning of the fourteenth century, some isolated Islamic thinkers, notably Ibn Khaldun (1332–1406), began to shift their attention to the actual situation in which a Caliphate consisted of a more or less loose confederation of independent provinces, each under a military leader as sultan or emir. They urged that the discussion of government must concern itself not with the Caliphate but with the province or kingdom (*mulk*) which alone had reality as a political and social unit. They suggested that the actual ruler (*malik*) should look to the inhabitants as his subjects, rather than as members of the wider community of the faithful, and should base the state, which alone provided a province with a degree of order, upon the effective support of men in that province. It was not until the seventeenth century, however, that this first advance towards the notion of sovereignty was followed up by other thinkers in the Muslim world. And not even in the twentieth century can it be said that this notion has made much headway in practice in the Islamic world against older tenacious ideas and unchanging social conditions.

By the time of Ibn Khaldun ideas similar to his had already emerged in Western Europe, where they were to develop in time into the notion of the sovereignty of the state. But before we consider that process we must next ask whether men attained to the notion of sovereignty over Western European Christendom as a whole before they began to develop it as a result of their growing preoccupation with the basis of authority in each of the several communities of which Christendom was composed. The answer to this question has been much debated. It depends on the extent to which Western Europe was, or was conceived to be, a single political society—on whether it approximated more to the conditions obtaining in Byzantium or more to those which obtained in the world of Islam—and this issue itself is not easy to settle because Europe's political development after the fall of Rome took place between the lines pursued at these other two extremes.

Experiencing, after the fall of Rome, a far more disastrous internal collapse than did Byzantium, Western Europe could not remain a unitary society. Inheriting, on the other hand, the impress of centuries of Roman unity and government and the Roman acceptance of the Christian religion—inheritances which were swept away in the areas of Islam's advance—it constituted a framework in which the effort to restore political unity was likely to be made, and in which that effort would be sustained by Roman ideas of rule. This effort was made by the rulers of segmentary kingdoms—by barbarian chiefs up to the establishment of Charlemagne's Empire; by a succession of German kings after an interval following Charlemagne's Empire's collapse. Their method was conquest but they used it within the shell, as it were, of Roman practices and theories, struggling to gain the title of Roman Emperor, or at least of Roman Emperor in the West, and invoking in their aid the memory, the conventions and the symbols of Roman government—including the phrases and terminology associated with the Roman idea of sovereignty. But in the conditions which actually prevailed after the replacement of Roman rule by tribal communities their struggle was of no avail and these symbols and phrases remained hollow and empty. And in these same conditions and most pronouncedly after Charlemagne's death at the beginning of the ninth century—when these separate communities began to consolidate on lines of their own; when the range of effective government had been drastically reduced; when the basis of the Empire had been shifted to the German area which had never been ruled by Rome; when the Empire's rule was restricted in practice to parts of the German and Italian areas and was even there acknowledged reluctantly, if acknowledged at all, by dukes and counts and princes—the history of the area entered upon a new phase in which such unity as was retained by Europe as a whole became primarily, if not solely, religious and ritual in character.

So much was this so that the possibility arose that Europe would develop into a single theocracy on the lines of Islam when it had lost the political unity which Byzantium managed to preserve. On the basis of a reform movement which sought to make Christianity more effective as the ground of religious unity, and on the basis of a parallel development of the Papacy as the increasingly effective head of the Church as an order, Christendom now replaced Europe and the Empire as the name for the area. The earlier tendency to regard Europe as the single world polity which had descended from the Roman Empire—a tendency which persisted into the tenth century—increasingly gave way to the disposition to think of the community of Christians as a universal Church or commonwealth which could know no distinction between the spiritual and the temporal spheres and which thus needed only one law and one government. And in the prevailing conditions, and given the fact that ritual supremacy is often accepted when political supremacy is impracticable or is opposed, it is only to be expected that the Papacy would claim —and that many would believe—that the only proper head of this single society was he who was already the ruler of its Church. From the eleventh century onwards there was a steady advance towards this full theocratic argument, by which the Pope ruled Christendom as an inheritance from St. Peter while the Emperor in Europe ruled only by a delegation from the Pope—and by which it was argued, on the basis of further fictions, that the Emperor in Byzantium ruled in his different way only by the connivance and volition of the Pope or only illegitimately over a kingdom of heretical Greeks.

In so far as it was uncontested—in the circles which accepted it—this theocratic argument constituted in itself a formidable barrier to the survival of any notion that Christendom as a whole was governed by a sovereign authority. Its logical outcome was not to establish the sovereignty of the Pope in the place of the sovereignty of the Emperor but to complete a structure of ideas in which the notion of sovereignty as such was, as in Islam, irrelevant. The Pope alone in this structure was free to decree what was right or in the public interest; and from the beginning of the eleventh century he was not bound in this by the decisions of his predecessors—he was irresponsibly supreme. But the Pope, like the Caliph, did not govern; and the law which he announced—the canon law— was not a law but a morality which recognized no distinction between the religious, political and social fields; not the law of any community but the norms applying in all the communities and valid throughout Christendom; not the law of an absolute Pope but the law of God which the Pope proclaimed and defended. Not for nothing has it been concluded that in its struggle with the Emperor from the eleventh century onward "the Papacy was not in its own eyes endeavouring to gain supreme power" but was "protecting the existing order against obstruction and infringement", and that "its supremacy, which was from God, was for this purpose".[1]

Even so, the papal theocratic argument could not come to dominate political thought and practice in Europe to the extent that it dominated in the Islamic world. It might be unanswerable to those who accepted its premises; but there were circumstances which made it impossible for all men to accept them—which made it certain that they would not be "always quite appreciated".[2] Foremost among these was the

[1] M. WILKS, *The Problem of Sovereignty in the Later Middle Ages* (1963), p. 46.
[2] W. ULLMANN, *Principles of Government and Politics in the Middle Ages* (1961), p. 63.

fact that the Emperor existed, and with him a vast accretion of imperial tradition and practice. His rulership was not built into the ecclesiastical hierarchy: it had been reconstituted before the papal argument developed and he was not made by the Pope from whom, from the end of the eighth century, he received his crown. The Pope might claim the right to depose him; but even the Papacy admitted that papal deposition did not relax the ties which bound his subjects to him. The Pope might claim to be able to effect this by excommunication. But it was one thing to assert that the Church had been committed to the Pope by St. Peter—though not even that assertion could be established on the evidence of the New Testament—and quite another thing to prove that rulership over the Church entailed rule over all life. Muslims sometimes described the Pope as the Caliph of the Franks, as the Latins often confused the political status of the Caliph with the primarily ecclesiastic position of the Pope. In truth, however, the Pope could be only the Caliph of the Messiah. Nothing that he could do could prevent Emperors from regarding his claim to be more than this as what it was in fact—"a usurpation of an established imperial right to rule".[1]

In this situation we might expect that the claims of the Emperor to be ruler of Christendom continued to involve the concept of sovereignty at this time when the Papacy aspired to the kind of supremacy which excluded it. Yet this was not the case. To begin with, it is true, the Western Emperor sought to perpetuate and build on this concept which had come down to him from Rome—and which remained effective in the Eastern Empire where, in combination with the unitary concept of the state, it had absorbed and dominated the theocratic implications of Christianity. It has been said that "the idea of a [separate] Roman Empire in the West was exclusively the intellectual off-spring of the Papacy",

[1] WILKS, op. cit., pp. 69–70.

from speculation about which "Charlemagne stood aloof".[1]
Whether we accept this or whether we believe, as seems equally plausible, that at least from the creation of Charlemagne's
extensive Empire the leading ruler in Europe had reasons
no less powerful than the Pope's for claiming the inheritance
of Rome—in terms of freedom from the universal claim of
Byzantium and of support in asserting his rule in his own
lands—there can be no gainsaying the importance which the
Emperors after Charlemagne long attached to the possession
of the imperial crown; to the argument that their Empire
was in direct descent from Rome's; to physical control over
the city of Rome; to such titles as *Imperator Romanorum et
Francorum, Romanorum Imperator, Rex Romanorum*; to copying
and imitating the imperial institutions, offices, emblems and
rites of Byzantium and ancient Rome. In the same way the
territorial expansion of the Emperor to the east—and even
against Byzantium itself—was increasingly undertaken from
the end of the eighth century with secular motives that were
but thinly disguised by the papal approval of the mission of
spreading Christianity to Slavs and Greeks. It was undertaken,
indeed, with motives and policies that are explicable only
within the framework of an aspiration to re-establish the unity
of the Roman-imperial dominion which sprang from the
continuing influence of the concept of Roman emperorship.[2]
Nor can it be doubted that in support of these policies the
language and the symbols of sovereignty were for long
preserved by imperialist scholars and *littérateurs*. But it is
equally plain that the imperial position increasingly lacked
after the collapse of the Carolingian Empire the attributes in
terms of power and acceptance which could alone have given
reality and relevance to these things.

[1] W. ULLMANN, "Reflections on the Medieval Empire", in *Transactions of
the Royal Historical Society*, 5th Series, Vol. XIV (1964), pp. 95–6.
[2] ULLMANN, loc. cit., pp. 99–103.

Perhaps the best proof of this may be seen in the fact that it was not by reference to a claim to sovereignty that imperialists defended themselves against the extension and application of papal theory after the middle of the eleventh century. Against the new papal claims—against the doctrine that the Pope inherited from St. Peter the total power which he could only delegate in part to the Emperor and to kings—imperialists rested their defence of the Emperor's independent title to rule upon the older papal defence against the domination of the Emperor—upon the doctrine of "the two swords". This older theory, the theory by which God delegated His power to the Pope in his sphere as He delegated it to the Emperor in his, was no less theocratic than the newer papal argument. It did not assert that the Empire was a different kind of community from that in which the Pope claimed to be supreme. It insisted only that the Emperor owed his position in Christendom directly to God, and not to God through the mediation of the Pope. Like the papal doctrine itself, it was a theory of rule but not a theory of rule involving the idea of sovereignty. The Investiture Contest was a struggle between two Popes.

How shall we explain this fact? It is sometimes said that the Emperor was impeded in his efforts to maintain a different, a secular, position by Byzantium's denial of his autonomy in Christendom. Certainly, Constantinople never yielded the claim to overlordship in the West which it deduced from its direct succession to ancient Rome. But this claim, coming from without, was even more artificial—even less accepted in Europe—than was the papal claim to the sole ultimate rulership of Christendom. This papal claim presented a more serious obstacle to the continuance of the idea of sovereignty of the Emperor because it was a challenge from within Christendom. But not even this explains why the Emperor fought it on papal or theocratic grounds. What needs to be taken into account is the fact that the papal challenge itself resulted from a vast if slow shift in conditions and ideas throughout Western Europe during the previous two and a half centuries from which the Emperor had not remained immune. Before the Pope could move to the claim for supremacy he had to escape the situation in which he owed his own position—as did the Patriarch in Constantinople and as was the practice in Christendom also until the eleventh century—to imperial appointment and protection. What enabled him to do so from the middle of the eleventh century, nearly three hundred years after he had established the basis of the claim by becoming the only lawful dispenser of the Western Imperial Crown, was the culmination of a great movement of religious revival and reform; and in the course of this movement, while the Church was developing as an organization and the Pope was becoming its increasingly effective head, the Emperor's position also became less secular and more theocratic. For it was not only as a result of the growing power and influence of the Church that the character of Christendom was changing sufficiently to generate a papal bid to convert it into a theocracy. If it was moving towards a greater emphasis on religion and a greater unity in ritual and in ecclesiastical organization, it was doing so in proportion to—perhaps, indeed, in consequence of—its slow departure ever since the collapse of the Carolingian Empire from the political relationships established under the unitary state of Rome towards the political conditions and relationships of a highly segmented, if still single, political society in which separate communities were evolving under the sway of a highly segmentary and largely nominal state.

It was this last development which constituted the underlying obstacle to the continuing validity—the main reason for the increasing artificiality—of the claim to a sovereign position by the Emperors. In the field of practice it is this which explains why the Emperors increasingly gave more attention to extending Christendom than to ruling it—or even to ruling the German area on which their main power was now based. They could in these circumstances more easily implement the more antique aspect of the ancient Roman Emperor's position —the tradition that he was *dominus mundi*, Lord of the World —than the more novel—the theory that he was above the law of a society in which he governed. In the field of ideas it is this which explains why they relied not on this more novel theory, despite their retention of the language and symbols which had once been associated with it, but on the Christian theme in which the whole of medieval thought was immersed. If he was not yet the complete enigma which he presented to the men of the Enlightenment, who dismissed him as neither Holy nor Roman nor an Emperor, the medieval Emperor was in fact failing from the outset to be either Roman or an Emperor, as Rome had understood that term, and was becoming the more Holy in the process. And so much was this so that when the Papal-Imperial struggle broke out it was so far as Christendom was concerned—if a distinction is made between the Emperor's capacity as Emperor in the West and his capacity as monarch in lands which formed but a part of Christendom—a struggle between two theocratic authorities for leadership in a ritual community rather than a conflict between secular and spiritual authorities for the government of a body politic.

The Absence of the Concept of Sovereignty in the Separate Communities of Medieval Europe

If Christendom as a whole was a collection of separate communities in some respects, even while remaining a single community in some others, and if this explains why Emperor and Pope came to share the same body of thought towards it, we must next ask whether this body of thought—this view of society as an instrument of salvation, of Christendom as a single society, of its head as the agent of God; and this uncertainty and controversy as to whether one or both of these heads ruled over the whole body of the faithful—was shared by rulers and other men within the separate communities of which Christendom consisted. The answer is not in doubt. While it did not constitute the totality of medieval ideas in politics—the actual division of Christendom was too pronounced for that to be possible—there was no theoretical, as opposed to *de facto*, resistance to the theocratic position of Pope and Emperor during the Middle Ages.

There was no such resistance to their conception of Christendom because conditions in each of the separate communities, no less than in Christendom as a whole, were such as to produce there a no less theocratic attitude to rule. On one level, no doubt, this was due to the pervasion of all thought by the Christian theme. But if we are to explain this pervasion we must understand this further point. Like Christendom as a whole in relation to the Emperor and the Pope, the separate communities were themselves segmented societies in terms of their own systems of rule. They were societies ruled often enough by a state but in each case by a segmentary state.

Wherever we look—from the extreme presented by ungoverned pre-Conquest England to the other extreme in the relatively highly integrated Anglo-Norman kingdom; from the German area, where the duchy divisions were so fundamental as to be almost incompatible with the existence of a German kingdom, to the French kingdom in which the theoretical strength of the centre withstood every actual excess of feudal disintegration—the variations in the degree of segmentation that we notice from time to time and from place to place pale into insignificance beside the fact that this was the chief characteristic of all the societies of medieval Europe. Although they had in most cases passed the tribal stage and were accustomed to the forms of the state from as early as the sixth century A.D., the association of a given area or boundary with any one state, of any particular society with any particular monarchy, was not everywhere guaranteed until a far later date: as Maitland said, "our medieval history will go astray, and our history of Germany and Italy will go far astray, unless we can suffer communities to acquire or lose the character of states somewhat easily . . . unless we know and feel that we must not thrust our modern 'state concept' upon the reluctant material".[1] Even in the more stable areas, where a society underwent continuous rule by the same state, the community fiercely insisted on confining the state to the passive and defensive role of maintaining existing rights and customs.

When a king pursued a programme of centralization in defiance of custom, or a foreign policy which departed from long tradition, he found that the magnates, who depended on the weakness of the centre for their own power, became his natural enemies. The magnates included his own relatives; for the political organization of the medieval community displayed another feature of the primitive state. Throneworthiness, the right to rule, remained the right of a royal kin, all of whose members possessed the throne. It was not until the thirteenth century, even in the most developed of the communities, that kin-right gave way even in practice to primogeniture and individual hereditary right in royal families. Alongside the kin-right of royal families, moreover, was a kin-right of the other nobilities, whose power rested on their status of nobility by birth. From the fall of the Carolingian Empire this segmentation had everywhere been formalized either by the development of the feudal system—the chief characteristic of which, in all the different degrees to which it developed, was the dispersal to magnates of regalian or government powers and not merely of landed property—or else—as under the German monarchy—by the victory of the baronial

[1] O. GIERKE, *Political Theories of the Middle Age* (Eng. trans., 1900), Introduction, p. ix.

argument that these powers had not been dispersed because they had never been centralized. Except in new-conquered lands like the England and the Sicily of the Normans this feudal dispersal had become hereditary, without a royal right of recall. It is not difficult in these circumstances to understand either the prevailing attitude to obedience—the conviction that those whose rights and customs were threatened by the Crown were authorized to resist—or the persistence of the right of self-help in the form of a vendetta in societies in which the Crown was unable to act or was prevented from acting.

In these circumstances, again, and given this prevailing attitude, only a ruthless and autocratic monarch could hope to increase the power and the resources of the state. But so great was the danger of rebellion and so small were the resources available to the state that few medieval kings made any serious inroad into the attitudes that went with the segmentary condition. It accordingly comes as no surprise that in their struggle against the limitations imposed on them by their communities they became as theocratic as the Pope and Emperor in their outlook upon rule. From Merovingian times, taking the title *Rex Dei Gratia*, they emphasized their position as the vice-regent, in the community, of God. And in so far as the kings of Europe did succeed in building up their position from the ninth century—by evolving the king's law alongside the community's law, by producing the king's peace in place of the folk-peace and the vendetta, by acquiring the sworn allegiance of their subjects, by inventing the new concept of High Treason, by claiming that the other wielders of power in the shape of nobility and clergy held their power in virtue of office conferred by the Crown—it was in their capacity as the consecrated representatives of God, dating their regnal years from their anointing and not from their accession, that they succeeded, no less than as a result of their ruthless use of power. At least until the eleventh century, indeed, the monarch combined two bodies. He was not only the physical, mortal agent of God but also the representative of a mystical entity which never died. He was *Rex et Sacerdos*.

It followed from this that the monarch could not think to challenge the theories or deny the pretensions of the universalist theocratic authorities. On the contrary, his adoption of the title *Rex Dei Gratia* opened the way to the mediation of the Pope, so that the sanction or at least the confirmation of the ecclesiastical authorities, under the growing control of the Pope, became everywhere a necessary factor at the accession of a new king, in the shape of his consecration. It is true that it also forced the Pope to concede that the office of king, as of the Emperor, was itself a loan from God. It is true that wherever the king was the real power in the community he did not fail to stress this fact, or scruple to ignore and evade papal and imperial claims. When these claims were in any case conflicting, and when power and opportunity settled most issues, there were few kings who did not even dispute the papal arguments—that the canon law was valid without royal consent; that the Pope could annul secular laws; that the Pope could depose monarchs, transfer kingdoms, forbid conquests, allocate new lands, invalidate treaties; that it was the king's duty to extirpate papally-defined heresies—just as most kings were ready to support these arguments when it suited them. If we concentrate less on the claims of the universalist theory, and more on actual political developments, we cannot doubt, indeed, that for these two reasons the introduction of royal consecration strengthened the monarch against Pope and Emperor rather than Pope and Emperor against the monarch.

In sanctifying the wielder of power by a religious rite the Church of course tried to reserve to itself the right to scrutinize and approve those who were raised to rule; but it was practically impossible for it to restrict consecration to men who were worthy in its eyes—or to prevent the actual domination of ecclesiastics by kings—so that consecration soon became the formal recognition by the Church of the man who had obtained the throne, whatever might be the worthiness of himself or of the way in which he had acquired it. It was not for nothing that after the eleventh century the Papacy, in its struggle for greater authority and higher standards, began to insist that consecration did not make the ruler a priest, and that from the twelfth century it began to exclude royal consecration from the sacraments of the Church. It was not for nothing, either, that the kings of Europe then continued to uphold the sacramental character of their anointing—the priestly character of their kingship— in spite of the opposition of the Church. But it was one thing to oppose the universalist authorities by evasion and the use of their own weapons, and quite another thing to denounce their pretensions and advance an alternative theory of rule. And as this last development sufficiently indicates, it was not yet necessary or possible for monarchs to take the latter course. On the one hand, even in the full theocratic theory Pope and Emperor could not issue orders but could only exhort and advise. On the other hand, a king could not repudiate the theocratic pretensions of these authorities without undermining the argument, on which he increasingly relied, that he himself was a divinely appointed ruler in his own community.

What was true of rulers was true as well of other men in the community. When the community had not yet left the segmentary stage and when, in addition, the Pope and the Emperor actually existed in Christendom, it was natural enough that their universalist claims to overlordship in the community should come to complement the community's defence of its rights and customs against the ruler. For the Church, as for a theocratic Emperor, the sole function of the ruler was to carry out divine commands; for the community the sole function of the ruler was to preserve existing rights. Since neither Church nor community recognized that the monarch had rights *sui generis*, the ecclesiastical theory of resistance to a sinful monarch and the community's insistence on its right of resistance to a defaulting monarch naturally tended to supplement each other. And all the more was this the case after the middle of the eleventh century. While the Church remained weak and the Papacy was undeveloped, it had been papal policy to support kings against the community's primitive resistance tendencies. From the eleventh century, however, with the movement of religious reform against lay conditions and with the attempt of the Papacy to escape lay control, ecclesiastical influence allied itself with the upholders of the secular right of resistance, who were themselves increasingly vociferous against monarchical centralization, and the result of the merger was to transform the primitive right of self-defence into a positive duty of disobedience defined by canon law.

If we again make a distinction between the development of theories and the history of medieval politics, a distinction which must be constantly borne in mind, we can see that in practice it was only rarely, and in special circumstances, that the alliance of external theocratic authority with community revolt completely gained the day in the struggle against the *de facto* strength and the theocratic position of the monarchies. Perhaps in no community except the acutely segmented German community did the actual power of the ruler—who was in any case also the Emperor—succumb to the combined onslaught of community resistance, in the form of ducal rebellion, and papal pretensions. But this alliance no doubt encouraged some circles in all the communities to continue to regard the Pope as the delegator of all power, the Emperor as the prototype of all lordship, and to assert that these external authorities could rightfully be appealed to in defence of the community or of individuals against the king in emergencies. The conflict between the English king John and his barons which culminated in the Magna Carta of 1215 provides an illustration of the behaviour which was typical in such circumstances. Both sides in this conflict appealed to the Pope as the superior court and, while John became the Pope's vassal and took the Cross in the hope of getting the Pope on his side, the commander of the baronial forces took the title of "Marshall of the Army of God and the Holy Church" when they decided to take the field.

It was not solely or even mainly in this way, moreover, that the communities, no less than their rulers, were debarred from escaping from theocratic attitudes to rule. The conjunction of segmentary conditions within the kingdoms with the powerful spread of Christianity and with all the other circumstances which underlay the existence of authorities claiming universal authority within Christendom—a conjunction which produced the theocratic aspirations of the kings themselves—led in every society to a profound desecularization of thought. A process set in by which the law of the community was conflated with God's law. The law which the ruler, as the elect of the community, bound himself to protect was initially a purely customary law of the kind which is characteristic of the early stages in the development of societies—the good old law which was a compound of ethics, religion and acquired private rights. This now became confused, though never wholly equated, with divine law. Men's minds being already set within this framework when conscious writing and thinking about law and government were renewed, and most of the thinking and writing being the work of clerics, the result was to accentuate, from the tenth century onwards, the belief that law was something which prevailed over both ruler and community. Language and ideas inherited from Rome to a different effect—to the effect that there was a law of the state which the ruler could create, or a public law which the community had erected against the ruler, or a public law over which the ruler was set in the interests of the community or in the interests of the state—were absorbed into the notion of the law as such. At least until the thirteenth century men recognized only this law, which knew no distinction between ideal law and positive law, between public rights and private rights, between legality and morality. They were ignorant of legislative or ordaining activity in the modern sense, either in the interest of the state or for the benefit of the community. Such new law as they made they thought of as only carrying out or restoring existing valid rules and established private rights. Such law as was written down they regarded as merely a fragment of the all-embracing law which was not superseded, only recovered or better stated, when a new need or an older charter—or even a forged "older" charter—caused more of it to come to be written down. And in this idea of the restoration of the law they found all the freedom they needed to alter and expand existing law to keep it in harmony with current needs and ideas.

In such a structure of thought, and in the conditions which underlay it, there was no room for the development of the concept of sovereignty. The conditions were compatible with —indeed, they brought about—the existence of an immense gap between practice and theory, between politics and law. In practice, because of the technical incapacity of the law and the actual inefficiency of government, force might often prevail and law would easily be managed to suit. But in theory all law, in the separate communities as in Christendom, was subsumed in the law of God and given a sanctity which placed it above all earthly authority; and it is in the world of theory that the concept of sovereignty must be sought. We could use modern terminology to say that God and the law were sovereign in the medieval community, but such terminology is wholly inappropriate to the political condition of the communities and to the medieval idea of law. Until, as the community changed its character, this whole fabric of thought was shattered—until the notion that monarch and community were both subordinate to a universal legal order had disappeared—men within the communities of which Christendom was composed could no more conceive of the legalized will of an absolute government or of the overriding right of the community itself than they could entertain such a concept, the concept of sovereignty, in relation to rule over Christendom as a whole.

The Prehistory of the Modern Concept

When we consider these medieval attitudes to rule and law we can see what changes were needed, in the community of Christendom or in the communities within Christendom, before that concept, properly defined, could arise. The law had to be clearly divided into divine (or natural) law and the positive law of the community; the law of God and the law of the community had to be consciously separated. And then, secondly, either the community itself or the ruler (the state) had to come to be regarded as being at least above the positive law, even if remaining subordinate to the divine or natural law.

We are tempted to add that before it could be thought of as sovereign the community or the state had also to be released from the sway of the divine or natural law. But a little reflection will show that the emergence of the concept did not depend on this further step. For a power to be judged to be sovereign it is no more essential that it should be released from all moral and ethical bonds than that it should be free from the limits set by practicability; as it may be regarded as sovereign even though it cannot physically achieve all it might desire, so it may be so regarded even when it is thought to be morally restrained. All that was needed in this direction before men could conceive of sovereignty was that the divine or natural law should become less comprehensive, less a matter of law and more a matter of ethics, less a structure upheld by some external authority, than it was to the medieval mind. This change, a change of degree, would follow naturally, if also slowly, once the distinction had been made between the divine law on the one hand and the positive law of the community on the other.

When we consider the history of political theory we can see that these changes were accomplished as early as the end of the thirteenth century. In themselves, indeed, the ideas which had by then become widely established were hardly new. If only in a vague outline, the notion that there is a public law of the state, distinct from both divine and private law, must be as old as the earliest emergence of the forms of the state. This notion had hitherto been clouded by the confusion of public with private law and rights, and by conflict of the emerging state with the community or the people; but it is clear that by the end of the thirteenth century at any rate, in Europe if not elsewhere, under the influence of the consolidation of government forms and powers but also assisted by the growing knowledge of Roman law and of Aristotle, it had acquired a quite new prominence and precision. In the separate communities of Europe by that date, no less than in the theories of the universal authorities, it was commonly recognized that the divine or natural law and the positive law were different, if complementary; that in the field of positive law the public law associated with the authority of the state (*status regis*) was different from the private law of subjects *inter se*; and that the government's power, being indispensable for the common weal or state of the realm (*status regni*) was superior, at least in emergencies, to human positive law and to private right. Governments regularly acted on these assumptions; and so commonly did they justify their acts with such doctrines as public necessity or public utility that the term *status regni* was used indiscriminately to signify either the public welfare or the public authority.

It remains arguable whether men had yet arrived at a true theory of the state—at the point where they could merge the state and the community in a single abstract conception that was also personified as the highest judicial entity. It is certain, however, that they had not yet evolved a theory of the state which involved the notion of sovereignty. On the contrary, as the history of politics reveals that they were still far short of the day when conflict between the public authority of the state and the private rights and privileges of the community would be an abnormal activity, so the history of political theory reveals that, despite the advances made on this level by the end of the thirteenth century, they were to produce no argued statement of a theory of sovereignty for nearly another three hundred years. If we study the political writings of this intervening period with any concern for precision we are left in no doubt that men now possessed the intellectual ingredients necessary for the notion of sovereign power—that, more than that, they frequently displayed the need or the wish to give expression to it—but that they did not succeed in stating it until the sixteenth century. Although the word "sovereignty" had gained currency by the beginning of that century, Bodin in his *Six livres de la république* of 1577 was perhaps the first man to state the theory behind the word.

How shall we explain this lag—this fact that, while men had the few basic ideas that are necessary for constructing the concept of sovereignty and even a desire to use them for that purpose, so that they produced many approximations to it, the concept evaded them for so long? We can say that it was due to the tenacity of medieval attitudes. But this is merely to restate the question—to ask why medieval beliefs were so persistent after the thirteenth century. The explanation seems to be that the political conditions which had underpinned the medieval structure of thought gave way but slowly, in a process that was less rapid than the reception of the new ideas, to political conditions in which these ideas could crystallize. And this for two reasons. The new ideas themselves were initially not so much the product of changes in Europe's political conditions as importations from another world, from a different civilization. And they were introduced into a Europe in which they could be used to strengthen existing political conditions as well as to undermine them, and thus to delay the completion of the political basis that was needed for a new framework of thought.

The ideas originated, were rediscovered, in a new familiarity with the writings of classical Greece and Rome. It was the revival of interest in Roman law, beginning in the twelfth century, which first led men to think of the positive law and the natural or divine law as being different things. This brought them face to face with the operations and the maxims of a state which had made law of its own free will for a body politic; it thus destroyed the medieval fiction by which new law was only the good old law restored. The rediscovery of Aristotle's writings, whose influence was widespread after about 1260, reinforced this lesson and also produced the further deduction that the body politic, or some authority within it, was supreme over positive law. For this taught men to regard the body politic, Aristotle's *polis*, as a purely human association and as the supreme human association, attaining its own ends by its own means. If these ideas now gained currency, if the very notion of politics as such now came as a novelty, if the language which went with it was revived—words like *Politikon*, for example, current in Byzantium but disused in Europe in earlier medieval times, were reintroduced—it was mainly as a result of this new knowledge of the classical world.

This is not to say that no changes were taking place in Europe's political and social conditions, or that changes in conditions were not in any case changing men's ideas. The twelfth and thirteenth centuries also saw the beginnings of a continuous quickening of social and economic activity in the communities of Europe, of a continuous improvement in communications and in organization, of an accompanying consolidation of the forms, institutions and habits of political association and of government. Who will deny, moreover, the interconnexion between these movements and the rapid spread of interest in the classical ideas? It is no coincidence that, although Europe owed the rediscovery of Aristotle to Islamic commentators, the work of Averroes and Avicena was far more influential in Europe than in the Islamic world. It provoked interest in Europe, as it failed to do in Islam itself, because only in Europe were these material developments simultaneously creating the political circumstances in which the new ideas could take firm root. In Islam, even after the rediscovery of Aristotle, thinkers like Ibn Khaldun remained isolated thinkers. In Europe, on the other hand, at least isolated thinkers, men like John of Salisbury and the occasional Roman or canon lawyer, knowing only the Latin literature, antici- pated by a whole century some of the message which men after 1260 were to derive from Aristotle's writings—argued as early as the middle of the twelfth century that the political community and its government were natural organizations, were a positive good rather than a necessary evil, were respectively the object and the subject of a human or positive law which must keep in line with the law of nature or of God but which was additionally necessary for the preservation of order and security. Then, again, the reception of Roman law itself was the more sure to take place in Europe, and was the more powerful as an instrument in the transition from medieval ideas of the law, because the increasing material and

F

political integration of Europe's communities was in any case beginning to emphasize the technical inadequacy of those ideas.

Although positive or statute law had long been superseding old law in practice, it was with the help of Roman law that men advanced to the principle that the positive law comprised the whole law, first in the sense that any statute could supersede all older law within its scope and subsequently to the extent that what was not written in a statute was not law. But such a principle was in any case coming to be required. The customary law or laws—fragmentary, limited to one locality and based on the assumption that each locality or individual could know the whole range of the legal order—had been effective enough while the community had consisted of the unconnected subcommunities of a segmentary society. It was not sufficient when, as was already the case by the thirteenth century, the segments were increasing their connexions, the central government was increasing its hold over all and men were stumbling upon the discovery that once they begin to promulgate some law they are driven on until they have promulgated a law that is comprehensive.

But if these changes had begun by the thirteenth century, and were already by then encouraging the spread of the classical ideas, it remains the case that men did not succeed before the sixteenth century in fashioning the new ideas into a consistent and effective body of thought. In some measure, no doubt, this was due to the fact that the classical texts themselves, in this like all other products of the human mind, contained no safeguards against confusion. The first impact of the revival of interest in Roman law was to give support to the advocates of existing authorities. It was not for nothing that the revival originated in the search of the Pope and the Emperor for precedents against each other when their rival theocratic arguments had reached a stalemate. But the rediscovery of Aristotle soon redressed the balance by providing arguments for those who wished to revitalize the doctrine of the supremacy of the popular will. Nor was this all. Roman law and Aristotelianism could each be used to buttress conflicting arguments. The Roman precedents enabled men to argue that authority was a delegation from the people, for this doctrine in the form of the *lex regia* had been among Roman formulas, but also to insist, by reference to the Roman maxims *quod principi placuit legis habet vigorem* and *princeps legibus solutus est*, that the *imperium* was above all human restraint. Aristotle suggested that the human community was a natural organization in its own right and that its government must be set over the positive law; but it was no less easy to use him in support of the medieval argument that the government should be subject to the law—to the superior law of God or to the basic rules of customary right, according to whether men equated Christendom or one of its component political communities to his *polis*.

It is not in the flexibility of the classical ideas and phrases, however, that we must look for the main reason for confusion and delay. This lay, on the contrary, in men's uncertainty as to which community was a *polis*, as to which authority possessed the *imperium*, and in their freedom to adopt in these matters varying equations between the formulas of the texts they had recovered and the political forms of their own day. For the classical ideas, introduced at a time when Europe's communities and authorities were in any case moving towards greater organization and centralization, and thus towards a growing preoccupation with the issue of ultimate authority as such, were also introduced at a time when the medieval proliferation of overlapping and conflicting communities and authorities had not yet been rationalized, let alone destroyed. It was one thing to formulate, as a result of the combination of the classical ideas and the movement towards greater organization, the elements of a new approach to political power: the separation of the law of the community from the law itself and the idea that the community or its ruler could not be subordinate to the community's law. When the actual political situation was still made up of overlapping and unfinished communities and of overlapping and conflicting authorities in each community, it was quite another thing to be able to fuse those elements into a wholly new synthesis.

Nor was this source of confusion soon to pass away. Up to the twelfth century Emperor and Pope, king and community, community and segment of community, church and state, all sharing the same medieval structure of beliefs, had each exploited the ideas of which that structure was composed, resisting each other and allying with each other as their separate interests dictated. In the long period of transition after the twelfth century all these forces continued to co-exist and, in their continuing struggle against each other, to turn to their own accounts the changes which were taking place in ideas, in conditions and in their own natures. It was on this account, as well as because the ordinary man will always resist the argument that justice is solely a matter of books and lawyers, that such medieval ideas as that which rested the right to resistance on the association of divine and customary law long persisted in the public mind. And if the new ideas were thus long confined to learned circles and government officials, it was for the same reason that even in these circles the new notions long co-existed with the more familiar doctrines of earlier times; that—what is more—older doctrines, which had hitherto been unargued statements of simple beliefs, were now erected into learned arguments, buttressed by the new ideas, under the influence of the scholarship and the disputation which had been released by the classical texts; and that the new ideas were themselves turned by diverse temperaments and conflicting interests to different ends. We should not be surprised that the result was not the rapid establishment of a new framework of thought about political power but a prolonged bedlam of incomplete and conflicting arguments.

A brief outline of the main schools of thought, as they developed from the twelfth century, will perhaps suffice to show that it was in this way that the notion of sovereignty eluded men. Extreme papalist writers and some of the Popes now asserted not merely—as the Papacy had asserted since Pope Gregory VII in the eleventh century—that the Pope must have the final word in a world where spiritual outweighed temporal considerations. They argued that he was an absolute personal ruler, as monarchically omni-competent as the classical Roman Emperor, in a Church which was the sole political community. Even they recoiled, however, from the implications of this argument; and these were not that the Pope was sovereign within Christendom. Because of the Pope's theocratic origin and his inability to desert it, they were that he was God Himself, reigning from outside and knowing no distinction between positive and divine law. His advocates also often contradicted themselves because their proposition conflicted with the actual situation. For the Church was manifestly not the sole political community— was not, indeed, a political community at all. From the outset, moreover, the papalists were confronted by men who were making use of the same classical precedents in the cause of the Emperors whom the Popes continued to crown. Just when the Papacy was first claiming (1157) that the Empire was a mere *beneficium*, held of an omni-competent Pope, the Emperors, using the findings of the school of Roman Law at Bologna, had resumed for the first time since Otto III at the end of the tenth century the imperial titles and the ancient language of their classical predecessors. And before long the imperialists insisting as urgently as the papalists that Christendom formed a single political community, began to reject the medieval defence of the Emperor's position within it—the view that he held his power directly from God, as did the Pope, in a double rulership—in favour of the argument that there could be only one ruler in this single community and that that ruler could only be the secular Roman Emperor.

The advocates of the Emperor were no more able than the Papacy, however, to state this claim in sovereignty terms, and this was for two main reasons. When the claim was made against the Papacy, against whom it was initially advanced, it conflicted with the theocratic traditions of the Empire as much as it did with the theocratic position of the Pope. At the very time when the Emperors were reviving the style and titles of the Roman Empire, in the middle of the twelfth century, the Emperor Frederick Barbarossa became the first medieval Emperor to adopt for the Empire the name *Sacrum Imperium* and to resort to that Emperor cult—that deification of the ruler—which had died after the eighth century with the victory of Christian attitudes to authority. This step was designed to make the Empire the equal of the Church on the Church's own ground; but it was incompatible with the notion of sovereignty because of its equation of the Emperor's law with the Law of God. Thus it was that, far from advancing beyond this theocratic framework after the twelfth century, under the influence of Roman Law, the Emperors continued to retreat from the position which Roman lawyers were constructing for them. By the middle of the fourteenth century they had abandoned the claim that they were the sole head in Christendom and had readopted as their official doctrine the medieval argument which was still upheld by most canon lawyers—the doctrine that the Emperor obtained his power direct from God in a dual vicariate with the Pope. And if the first reason for this was that the Emperors were unable to escape from their own theocratic past in their struggle with another theocratic universal authority, the other was that the Roman lawyers failed to provide them with a satisfactory alternative to theocratic arguments in relation to the other political authorities in a Europe that was not a single society.

For a century after they had begun to use Roman law to strengthen their claim for total power as against the Pope the Emperors still clung to a segmentary view of their power over these other authorities—the kings of Christendom, the princes in Germany, the cities of Italy. They maintained only that they held a superiority, a limited *potestas* of which the rights were conditioned by the Emperor's fulfilment of his duties. In a Europe that was becoming ever more segmentary, when regarded as a single community, this was all that the Emperor, when regarded as the ruler of this single community, could in fact maintain. In the same period, partly for this reason and partly because their attention was focused on their battle with the ideas of the Papacy, the Roman law supporters of the Empire similarly limited their claims on its behalf as against the regional rulers. They insisted, of course, that the Emperor was the sole universal authority and that the Empire alone was a true *Respublica* with a true public law. But they were disposed to admit that the Empire had in fact become divided, that some peoples did not use Roman law, that the separate kingdom was a *respublica* in some limited sense. They thus stopped short of pressing the Roman law concept of the *imperium* to its logical extreme and were content with tortured arguments like that by which the French, while they were not vassals of the Emperor, were nevertheless his subjects because they had once been incorporated in the Empire of Justinian. It was not until the end of the thirteenth century indeed that, in their anxiety to place legal obstacles in the path of any further alienation of the universal secular *imperium*, they began to go further in this direction than the Emperors themselves had gone. But as soon as they made this advance, denying at last the right or duty of resistance to the Emperor and insisting that not even he himself could reduce the Empire by gift or sale, they uncovered the real difficulty confronting them—the inapplicability of the Roman doctrine of the legal sovereignty of the *imperium* in the conditions of their time. It was the fact that other authorities were increasingly using their own Roman law arguments against the Emperor's supremacy which forced them to become more emphatic in their defence of the Emperor's legal supremacy. And what resulted from their greater emphasis on the Emperor's power was a type of argument that was even more tortured than that to which they had already been driven.

Ever since the end of the twelfth century, perhaps because of their desire to belittle the Empire and to defend the papal supremacy against its attack, some canon lawyers and some Popes had been more forward than the Roman lawyers in recognizing at least the *de facto* independence of the regional authority as against the Emperor. From at least the same date, as we shall see, some regional rulers and their propagandists had been no less backward in making the same claim. These assertions had owed nothing to the influence of Roman law. When Innocent III announced in 1202 that the King of France recognized no superior in temporal affairs, or when a canon lawyer agreed that the regional king was *de facto* independent of the Empire, the object was to advance the argument that Emperor and king were equally subject to the theocratic Pope and the law of the universal Church. When as early—or perhaps we should say as late—as the twelfth century the King of Spain or France or England announced that he was an emperor, or otherwise implied that he was independent of the universal Emperor, he was not calling in the Roman law to his aid or defying the Emperor of Christendom. He was giving expression to his ambitions in the imperial terms that came naturally to a primitive state which hardly knew, as yet, that the

Emperor existed. But from about the middle of the thirteenth century the Crowns and their propagandists in the main regional monarchies began to announce that they were independent of the universal Empire, that they were independent of it *de jure* as well as *de facto*, and they now based this claim on their own reading of the Roman law.

It was this development which drove the Roman law defenders of the Emperor to make, at last, the fullest claims for the total power of the universal *imperium*. But it was also on the same account that these claims now lost all resemblance to the classical imperial pretensions from which they were derived. Bartolus (1314–57) provides a good example of the predicament which now faced the Roman lawyers, and that in two ways. He himself, in the first place, was both an advocate of imperial claims and a consultant to Italian cities which had long exercised executive and legislative powers inconsistent with the Roman law definition of the imperial authority and which, like the kingdoms, were now claiming even *de jure* independence, a *plenitudo potestatis*. Then, secondly, though they are especially instructive because of his double role, his arguments are typical of those to which these men were reduced by the effort to square reality with the imperial power of the Roman law books, a power to which all cities had been subordinate. He first distinguished the independent city as a special case among the cities of Roman law: it was a *civitas* which acknowledged no superior, and thus a law unto itself. He then explained that such a city was still part of the Empire because it had acquired its rights by the overt or tacit consent of the Emperor, and thus held them of him in some *de jure* sense. But how could its rights and powers be distinguished either from those of the Emperor or from those of other cities which still acknowledged the Emperor while actually exercising the same independent powers? This problem he solved by dividing the imperial power according to the dignity and territorial expanse of the authorities exercising it. The power of the ordinary city was of the lowest dignity. That of the independent city was of a higher dignity but not, since it was limited to a single territory, of the highest. The power of the Emperor was highest in dignity because its expanse was universal—even though he did not exercise it within the city. The Emperor was ruler of the whole but not the ruler of the parts. "I say that the Emperor is truly lord of the entire world. And this does not prevent that others should be lords in a more particular sense, because the world is a kind of *universitas,* and hence there may be a person who possesses the said *universitas* and yet the individual things do not belong to him."[1]

It would be wrong to smile at these arguments. They represented a reasonably close approximation to the convictions which were to shape for a long time yet the political behaviour of even the forces which opposed the Empire's claims. But they illustrate how even Roman lawyers among the imperialists found it quite impossible to think of the *imperium,* let alone of any other power, in terms of sovereignty —how, instead of approaching the necessary identification of political authority with the political community, they were forced to equate the remote control of the greatest number of communities with supremacy. And they also help to explain why other supporters of the Emperor, and the Emperors themselves, preferred to rest their case on the Empire's theocratic traditions as well as on Roman law.

These traditions also resisted, again for understandable reasons, the aid of another school of thought which transcended, or which at least sought to terminate, the old papal–imperial struggle by totally rejecting, if only in its papal form at first, the theocratic outlook. From the end of the thirteenth

[1] Quoted in J. H. FRANKLIN, *Jean Bodin and the Sixteenth-century Revolution in the Methodology of Law and History* (Columbia, 1963), p. 15.

century, in reaction to the extreme papalists and under Aristotle's influence, anti-papal thinkers—Dante, Marsilius of Padua, William of Ockham, Nicholas of Cusa—asserted not merely that the Church was not the sole political community but that it was not a political community at all. It was simply the body of the faithful; and its head, the Pope, was a mere administrator of sacraments who could have no power and make no laws in temporal fields. And more than that, they denied the divine origin of the Pope's authority in the Church and urged that even in spiritual matters he should be subjected to the authority of a Council of the Church or of a Council of ecclesiastical and lay leaders. In the prevailing political situation these ideas made them, as we shall see, allies of the imperialists—who welcomed in their turn the argument that the lay power must be free from papal control in the lay sphere and that the lay power in a society should help to control the Church. But they were always embarrassing allies. For it was an easy step from the thesis that the Pope did not get his power from God to the argument that the Emperor did not get his power from God; from the thesis that the Pope should be controlled by a Council to the argument that all rulers got their power only from the society, the people, they ruled; from the thesis that the Church was not a political community to the argument that Christendom or the Empire was not a political community. And against these dangers on the level of thought, no less than against the obstacle which existed in politics, it was understandable that the Emperor and his defenders would retreat to the theocratic framework which they shared with the Popes who had hitherto been their primary enemy.

These anti-papal writers thus contributed little to the development of imperialist political thought. But they themselves, who might be expected to have approached more closely to a doctrine of sovereignty, were scarcely more successful in providing a new synthesis than were the various supporters of the Emperor and the Pope. Of the three arguments implicit in their anti-papal thesis, they advanced with varying degrees of clarity and emphasis to the first and the second, asserting that no political authority could hold its power of God and insisting that it was a rule of natural law that the rights of society, of the ruled, were the basis of all political power or at least of popular participation in government. But despite their recognition that men were in practice governed in regional kingdoms they could not yet advance to the third—to the belief that Christendom was not a single political community. On the contrary, the more they denied that the Pope ruled Christendom the more they needed to bring forward the Emperor and, ignoring the reversion of imperialists to theocracy, to invest him with non-theocratic authority—with that kind of authority which some of his own defenders were deriving from Roman law but from which others among his defenders were now shrinking. This was because their inability to rid themselves of the conviction that the Empire was, or ought to be, a single structure of rule was no less marked than their conviction that as single structure of rule required a single omni-competent and secular authority. If from the fourteenth century the medieval Empire, as Maitland said, "laboured under the weight of an incongruously simple theory [which] ... taught that the Kaiser was the *princeps* of Justinian's Law Books",[1] it was also propped up by this argument which resulted from the conjunction of the Christendom tradition and Greek political thought.

Thus Dante moved on from anti-papalism to insist in *Monarchia* (c. 1310) that if, indeed, the Emperor no longer ruled all men, as the Roman Emperor had once ruled them, then it was imperative that he should be restored to that

[1] O. GIERKE, *Political Theories of the Middle Age*, Introduction by F. W. Maitland, p. x.

position. For him that position was still one in which the Emperor, who could not delegate any part of his power, was a universal ruler who combined the competence of a lay ruler with that of a Pope. He was inconsistent, indeed, in saying sometimes that the Emperor and the Pope were completely separate, sometimes that the Emperor was not free from papal control in the spiritual field, and sometimes that the Emperor himself should have the powers of the Pope. Marsilius, writing twenty years later, was more decidedly anti-theocratic and more disposed to accept that men were divided into several kingdoms. For him the legislator in any community must be the people—even if he meant by the people only the magnates and especially the princes of the Empire who stood between the population and the ruler, in the same way as he held that the right of conciliar control of the Pope belonged only to the clergy and the lay rulers and not to the whole body of the faithful. For him the equivalent of the *polis* of Aristotle was without question the individual *regnum* or *civitas* of the Europe of his day. Yet even he maintained that the society of Christians, as opposed to other groups of men, was in some respects a single society which needed a single superior, that Christendom was a plurality which also constituted a unity; and thus he thought that the Emperor was the *pars principans* in the government of each *regnum* or *civitas*. Throughout his book *Defensor Pacis*, again, he used Christian and Roman, as did Dante, as interchangeable terms, believing that the population of Rome still acclaimed and legitimized the Emperor on behalf of all Christians. William of Ockham similarly perpetuated this tradition, which did not die until the second half of the fourteenth century. Like Dante he thought of the Emperor as being also a Pope who could depose kings and appoint kings to new provinces. Like Dante and Bartolus he insisted on the indestructibility of the Empire and the inviolability of the power of the Emperor—even though, like Marsilius, he based himself not on Roman law but on the argument that the Emperor had obligations to the people which he could not surrender without the people's universal consent. And not unlike Bartolus, in an attempt to provide a workable accommodation between the Emperor and the kings, as head and members of a single community, he made a distinction between the ordinary power of the Emperor, which he shared equally with the kings, and the emergency or reserve power of the Emperor, which was absolute.

With these radical humanists, then, as with the Roman lawyers, the obstacle which obscured the concept of sovereignty was not, as it was with the protagonists of the Pope and the theocratic defenders of the Empire, an impediment involved in their arguments as such. It was one which arose from the conflict between their arguments and the political conditions of the Europe of their day. By their arguments they were led directly enough to the notion that a body politic existed to serve the interests of men, and to promote justice and peace among them, and also to the notion that a supreme power was necessary in the body politic for this purpose. If they were deflected from the full implications of these notions it was not by the fact that they also regarded the supreme power as subject to the natural law and urged that the delegation of that power from the people was a principle of the natural law. The barrier which they could not surmount arose from their assumption that Christendom was a body politic in which the Emperor retained supremacy. It was on this account that they withheld sovereignty from Christendom's component communities while imposing upon its imperial superstructure an omni-competence which—partly because of the Empire's theocratic base and partly because of the hard reality underlying that base, the fact that the Emperor did not rule in the communities themselves—could not be stated in sovereignty terms.

This being so, and as it was already questionable whether the Empire could bear the strain of even this conception of its power, it might be expected that the obstacle of Christendom would present no problem to another school of writers—the national and above all the French publicists who were turning the new lines of thought to the advantage of the regional monarchies. But this was not the case. These men—Bracton, Dubois, Nogaret, King Philip IV—had no difficulty in announcing with imperialists and anti-papalists that the Pope had no jurisdiction within the kingdom, even in spiritual affairs. They naturally accepted the argument of the humanists that men were ruled in regional kingdoms by rulers who were in fact independent of external authority in temporal, no less than in spiritual, affairs. Yet they no more pressed this second argument to the point of completely denying the jurisdiction of the Emperor over Christendom than did men like Marsilius and Ockham. This was partly because the Emperor, lacking the executive arm within the kingdom which the Pope possessed in the shape of the clergy, was a theoretical overlord merely, and not an ever-present and active rival. But it was also due to the fact that for these men, no less than for Dante or Marsilius or Ockham, the universal society of Christians remained a single community of which France, for example, was a component part—that in some sense, indeed, Christendom had become more of a reality for them than it had been previously.

From the middle of the thirteenth century the resort of the national writers to Roman law enabled them to state more emphatically than ever before what kings and their spokesmen —what even Popes and canon lawyers—had been saying for at least half a century: that in temporal matters the king had no equal, let alone any superior, within his realm. Thus Bracton in England and his contemporaries in France maintained from that date, with the aid of Roman law, that the

king within the kingdom had of right all the attributes—
including the power to interpret the law and to make new
law—which, on the basis of the same Roman law but in
relation to all Christendom, the Roman lawyers were claiming
for the Emperor and the canon lawyers were claiming for the
Pope. But by that time imperialists had been making use of
Roman law in the interests of the Emperor for upwards of a
century; papalist arguments and the improved organization
of the Church had for just as long been advancing the claims
of the Pope; and the quickening of economic, social and
intellectual activity in Europe had conspired with these other
developments to produce in men's minds a greater consciousness of belonging to a universal Christendom even while it
had also generated a greater consciousness that the regional
communities were distinct communities. There seems little
doubt that it is this contradictory situation which explains the
uncertainty of the attitude of the French Crown towards
Roman law. In 1219 it had welcomed—indeed, it had
engineered—a papal ban on the teaching in the University of
Paris of that Roman law which the advocates of the independence of the French Crown were soon to exploit to such good
effect. In the same way, because of the danger that it would
strengthen the Emperor, Roman law was not known by its
own name in France but was called the *droit écrit*. But it also
seems highly probable, on the other hand, that it was on
account of the same contradictory situation that Bracton
stopped short of calling the King of England an Emperor;
that his French contemporaries could declare at one and the
same time both that the king legally possessed the *imperium*
within his realm and that the Emperor, while his jurisdiction
did not extend to the special realm of France, remained
dominus mundi; and that from the later years of the thirteenth
century the formula *rex imperator in regno suo* (the king is
Emperor within his own kingdom) became a characteristic

device for defending the leading monarchies against the imperialists' claims.

There has been much disagreement about the significance of this formula. Some scholars have maintained that it involved the claim that the regional Crown was completely independent of the Emperor in all respects. Others have argued that it conveyed only the assertion that, while remaining subject to the Emperor in the sense that the public law and public rights within the realm were held by delegation from the Emperor, the Crown was superior to all authorities in its own kingdom. This controversy would fall to the ground if it were supposed that the formula was invented by men who were anxious to claim that the king was *de jure* completely independent of the Emperor *within the kingdom* but who did not think or wish to deny the subordination of the king to the Emperor in affairs *affecting Christendom as a whole*. The king is wholly independent within the realm although there is an Emperor with undoubted powers over Christendom as a whole—this would then be the point of the phrase. And the fact that this is a reasonable supposition is suggested not only by the thought that such phraseology would be the only phraseology available to men who in these circumstances were trying to discriminate for the first time between the claims of a universal Empire within the separate kingdom and the claims of such an Empire in what we would today call its international role, but also by two other considerations.

These men had other formulas which they did not hesitate to use in relation to the king's internal powers and which unmistakably advanced the claim that the king was *de jure* independent in internal affairs—formulas like *rex superiorem non recognoscens* (the king recognizes no superior). And then, again, as we shall see when we turn to the development of the idea of sovereignty in the history of relations between states, there is no difficulty in explaining why they nevertheless did not deny the authority of the universal Emperor in universal affairs. Either they did not know how to do so because the forces upholding the tradition of a united Christendom were still too strong. Or they did not wish to do so because they were beginning to covet this authority for their own kings. It is not for nothing that it was just at this time that the kings in the separate kingdoms of Europe, who had previously been inclined to declare from time to time that they were Emperors in their realms even as the Emperor himself was Emperor in his, began to argue instead that they had as much right as the king in Germany to be elected into the single Emperorship of Christendom which they now recognized.

If only because it was extremely difficult to express and sustain such a distinction between the internal and the international competence of a universal authority, the obstacle of the Emperor was itself sufficient to prevent these writers from stating the claim to the independence of the Crown within the realm in terms of sovereignty. But there was another obstacle, equally serious, to their ability to advance thus far. If they were anxious to establish the independence of the Crown in relation to the universal authorities, they were also interested in establishing the omni-competence of the Crown in relation to other powers within the kingdom. If they used the Roman law and the *rex imperator* formula against the Emperor and the Pope, they used them also, from the thirteenth century, for the furtherance of the claims of the Crown against the attitudes of other authorities within the regional community, which was still a segmentary community to which the Roman law notion of royal omni-competence was an alien notion. The resort to it by the Crowns and their advocates was as often a defensive as it was an expansionist device, moreover, the aim being not so much to assert the omni-competence of the Crown as to place legal obstacles in the way of the further alienation of regalian rights to the nobilities among whom so many of these rights were already distributed. For as well as being segmentary, and as well as it being the case that their segmentation was highly regularized in a feudal system in proportion as the community itself was highly developed, these communities were now asserting their rights against the monarchies more powerfully than ever before, and as powerfully as the monarchies were asserting themselves within the communities and against the Pope and the Emperor.

They were doing so on the basis of a network of customs and traditions which had as yet been in no way weakened by the passage of time. We shall soon have to discuss the character of these traditions and to describe their significance for the future development of the idea of sovereignty. For the present it is enough to emphasize that they were now achieving increased prominence because the communities, no less than the Crowns, were becoming increasingly organized and integrated. It was on this account, because circumstances were producing both the desire for greater powers on the part of the Crown and the possibility of more effective resistance on the part of the community, that there took place from the thirteenth century in the more developed societies a rapid development of constitutional procedures and ideas. Its effect was to circumscribe the rights, if not always the powers, of the Crowns by giving precise formulation to what had hitherto been vague, if powerful, limits. When the king had by long custom no right to tax without consent unless the tax was traditional, the community now fixed and settled the traditional limits beyond which it would not yield without compensating concessions by the Crown. When by long established theory he governed and legislated as the mouthpiece of the community, with its consent, the rules and procedures for obtaining that consent, previously elastic and undeveloped, were now formalized by the organization of Parliaments and Estates in the interests of the magnates who were in fact increasing their powers. When the combination of custom and regional autonomy had long placed numerous other limits upon his freedom of action—such as his inability to order his subjects to serve beyond the realm or even outside their own provinces "without the king's wages", or unless the king was present in person—men set greater store upon their rights, and sought to place them on a contract basis, in proportion as the Crown experienced a growing interest in circumventing them.

Already before the end of the thirteenth century men who maintained, like Bracton, that the king had no equal or superior in some respects—in reference to the universal authorities particularly, but also possibly in an executive sphere which they were trying to distinguish from the sphere of legislation—also insisted that the king could not make or modify laws without the agreement of his barons. And against this background, and given the further stimulus of the fact that other men were using the classical ideas to claim supremacy for the Pope or the Emperor or the King, it was not long before some men began to urge that the meaning of the Roman *lex regia* was that supremacy resided rather in the community in the sense that the original right of the People had been transferred to the monarch only as the temporary concession of an office which the People could at any time revoke—in the sense that the community was always the true and permanent repository of power whatever the form of government, and thus possessed a continuing legislative control over the acts of government. During the fourteenth and fifteenth centuries there was an ever-increasing recourse to these views in defence of the rights of Estates against the monarchies as these, rather than the magnates and the provinces, began to grow in power.

We can be sure that this internal situation within the kingdoms was no less important than the problem posed by the existence of the Emperor and the Pope in delaying the claim by the monarchies to the possession of an absolute legal power within their kingdoms. When we consider the existence of both obstacles to the advancement of such a claim we can easily understand why kings stopped short of using even the title "His Majesty"—which was restricted to the Emperor until, in the sixteenth century, it was appropriated for themselves by Francis I in France, Philip II in Spain and Henry VIII in England. But just as the advocates of ruler supremacy within the kingdoms tempered their doctrines with the recognition that the king could not legally overstep the customary limits of his office, that he had only rights conditioned by duties and thus a limited power, so the advocates of the supremacy of the community in the persons of its representatives similarly limited their claims. These resulted in no more than a more precise statement of the community's ancient right to resist an illegal king. An earlier vague right and duty of resistance to illegality was reformulated as a doctrine by which every command which exceeded the limits of the ruler's authority was a nullity impairing *his* fundamental right, so that no man could be obliged to obey it and all men were entitled to compel the ruler to abide by the law—and sometimes as a right of resistance by which tyrannicide was justifiable or at least excusable. Not even the most extreme proponent of these doctrines failed, however, to make a distinction between the king's person, which could be resisted, and the Crown, which was beyond attack, or denied that even in his person the ruler obtained from the original contract an independent right of lordship from which he could not be deprived so long as he was true to his pact. On the popular no less than on the monarchical side the prevailing framework of thought remained one in which authority was held in common by the community and the ruler.

Nor was it only as a result of being thus divided that

authority, in the prevailing attitude, fell short of the conception of an absolute power within the society. It was consistent with—indeed, it was essential to—this attitude that the natural or divine law which was above ruler and community retained great prominence in the outlook of both schools of thought. Differences inevitably arose as to boundaries in the exercise of this divided authority, and especially as to how far and on what grounds the ruler might modify or abrogate private and community rights without exceeding his legal powers. These differences were partly solved by the growth of the distinction between the legislative and the executive functions in the state, but they could not thereby be avoided. And in this situation the characteristic arguments on both sides were arguments which emphasized the binding force of an external law. Subjects sought security against the Crown by grounding their rights—and especially those in property and from the contract with government—in natural law, which placed them above the reach of positive law, of statute, of the state. The Crown supplemented its growing insistence that the rights and the powers acquired by parliaments were privileges arising from positive law, conceded by the state and freely revocable by the ruler, with an equally marked insistence that kings were God's agents who could not alienate their powers. Nor did it omit to claim that the state, being the essential attribute of a community, was itself grounded in natural law, was possessed of an immutable sphere of action, and thus exercised rights which needed no title in positive law and which could not be diminished by that law.

In these doctrines that were developed by and on behalf of monarchs we have the germs of the idea of state sovereignty in the form in which it would later emerge. It cannot be doubted, moreover, that before the end of the Middle Ages men were familiar with them—were familiar, for example, with the argument that every act or contract which sacrificed the essential right of the ruler or the state was void, and with the argument that no title could give protection against the claim to submission which flowed from royal or state power. They are properly seen, nevertheless, as deductions from the main framework of political thought which could not achieve independent standing, practical validity or general currency until that framework had further dissolved. And it was not until this process of dissolution had culminated in the revolutions in thought and politics of the period of the Reformation that they moved to the forefront, as can be seen from the fact that the most influential school of ideas from the thirteenth century until that time, a school whose influence few other writers and thinkers escaped, was not among those whose doctrines have so far been surveyed, but was that of St. Thomas Aquinas.

For the characteristic doctrine of Aquinas and his moderate humanist followers, the Thomists, was not the belief which created so many problems for the more extreme advocates of the various conflicting powers: the belief that some one of these powers was or ought to be the superior or the omni-competent authority. It was the denial that Christendom or any of its component communities harboured or required an authority of this kind. The Thomists denied such power to Pope and Emperor, both against each other and as against the kingdoms of Christendom, from a determination to terminate the rivalry of these authorities in a balanced system in which all were retained. In reaction to extreme papalist claims they held that no Pope could make laws which led to sinful conduct, or which disturbed the peace of a kingdom, and that disobedience to papal command, and even the disciplining of the Pope by the lay authorities, was lawful if dictated by conscience—for the substance of the divine or natural law was unalterably fixed by God, the Bible was to be preferred to the Pope as the authority even in religion, and the kingdom was a natural human community set up by God for the maintenance of order. In reaction to extreme imperialist claims they denied such power also to the Emperor of Christendom, pointing out that his normal executive authority was limited, like any other king's, to his immediate territories. At the same time, they retained the belief in Christendom as a single society, and as one in which both Pope and Emperor had a place, and sought to reconcile the *de jure* universality of papal-imperial rule with the *de facto* existence of regional kingdoms in two ways.

In the first place they held that the world-authority of Pope and Emperor did not normally conflict with the freedom of the regional ruler because the authority of these universal authorities was in the nature of an emergency power alongside the normal authority of themselves and other rulers. Thus they held that the Pope retained a *plenitudo potestatis* to which the lay authorities were subject in emergencies, even as the Pope might become subject to their jurisdiction if he became a tyrant. Then again, not unlike Dante or Ockham, they held that a just war, being an exceptional step in the public good, could be declared only with papal-imperial consent, *auctoritate papae et imperatoris*, since Pope and Emperor together were the supreme arbiters in peace and war, the prince of peace, *princeps pacis*. In the second place, their recognition of the independence of regional kings and their insistence that the kingdom was a natural community did not persuade them that monarchical authority differed in quality from that of the universal authorities. On the contrary, they stressed its similarity to the normally restricted power of the Emperor in the single society to which the kingdoms belonged.

If the society of Christendom was seen as being a federation of semi-autonomous kingdoms so was each kingdom regarded as being in its internal structure a network of adjacent semi-independent rights. Its over-all government by the king was compatible with the fact that lords and magnates remained supreme in their own estates, just as the existence of the universal authorities was reconcilable with that of separate kingdoms: the two would normally work in harmony by staying in their own spheres; and the necessary right of the king occasionally to step beyond his sphere was balanced by the occasional right of subjects to resist his actions if they were illegal. When some men argued with regard to power in the kingdom that it came from God through the ruler, and others urged that it could come only from the People, the Thomists again sought to synthesize these conflicting doctrines. In the kingdom, as in Christendom as a whole, a mixed system prevailed or ought to prevail—a system in which the powers of the ruler were rightly seen as coming both from God and from the People, since full power had originally lain both in the ruler as God's agent and in the community; a system in which the ruler was supreme in some contingencies and the ruled were supreme in others; a system which could sustain a judicious balance of monarchical, aristocratic and democratic elements in the working of the body politic; a system which varied, moreover, from community to community, as being the *regimen politicum et regale* standing between the *regimen regale* of universally valid natural law which came from God and the *regimen politicum* which was set up by the varying positive laws of different communities.

Some scholars have seen in this thesis, with its argument that the ruler's limited or emergency absolute power for the common good was balanced by a similar right in the whole community to act extra-legally in emergency conditions if the public weal required it, the beginnings of the new notion that the body politic was vested with personality of its own, over and above the rights of ruler or subjects. But in fact there was nothing new in the concept of the public weal as such, nor would this ancient concept acquire new significance until

Machiavelli advanced the principle of *raison d'état* by permitting the ruler the right to do what he pleased for the good of the community while denying the community the same right against the ruler. When he based this right on the interests of the community, instead of on the divine justification for it which the Thomist thesis retained, Machiavelli also took a step towards the concept of sovereignty. But this concept was as far beyond the reach of the Thomists as was Machiavelli's understanding of the body politic. If any authority was sovereign in their scheme, it was God alone. Within the community ruler and ruled had each renounced their absolute power to Him, as within Christendom the emergency power of Pope and Emperor was His power.

In this respect, indeed, their great attempt to combine Aristotelianism with the Christian cosmology—their effort to build a bridge between Pope and Emperor, between the universal society and the developing regional communities, and within these communities between the rulers and the ruled—was a bold synthesis of the political realities, no less than of the intellectual convictions, of the time. It was not for nothing, for example, that it took over from men like Bracton and Beaumanoir, who were struggling to combine Roman law with customary law and the procedures of feudalism in Europe's societies, the argument that legislation was a joint affair between ruler and ruled, in the sense that the ruler alone could summon the Estates but that it was not in his power to refuse to do so. The doctrine, again, that the ruler was above the law in the sense that he could dispense with it in exceptional circumstances, as the vicar of God and the agent of the natural law, but that he was below it in the sense that he had normally to operate within the bounds of the law of the land, which was also his own law—so that his occasional right to act contrary to liberties and customs was counterbalanced by an emergency right of the community to act against him—

faithfully reflected the actual balance of rights and power which prevailed in many of the kingdoms.

Equally clearly, however, the Thomists also built this complex structure of political theory from a conscious anxiety to avoid the conflicts which were sure to arise in the circumstances of the time from any attempt to press into practice a more uncompromising, a more absolute, conception of political power. It is this fact which explains in the last resort their view that ultimate authority was not to be realized in universal or in regional authority, in church or in state, in ruler or in ruled—in any concrete or human form, indeed—but was rather to be conceived of as far as possible in abstract terms.

It was, no doubt, for both of these reasons that few writers and thinkers escaped the influence of this synthesis during the thirteenth, fourteenth and fifteenth centuries. If during all that time the majority of men adhered to a belief in the oneness of mankind but also to the conviction that this oneness was best expressed through a plurality of overlapping authorities, if they thus subscribed to a conception of the political world by which it consisted of a federative hierarchy—of a spectrum of powers stretching from village and city through province and then through kingdom to the Empire and the Papacy which were the visible embodiment in Christendom of God and the natural law—this was partly because this conception corresponded with the actual distribution and forms of power within each kingdom and in Christendom as a whole. But it was also partly due to the fact that the main concern of most men was the struggle to keep this plurality of authorities in that correct relationship which they thought necessary for the preservation of the *harmonia mundi*, the peace of the world. For changes in Europe's actual condition during all this time were constituting an ever-growing threat to this harmony as well as placing an ever-increasing strain upon this outlook.

The Emergence of the Theory of the Sovereignty of the Ruler

The most prominent of these changes, the shift of emphasis which finally shattered this belief in a hierarchy of authorities and this resulting attitude to authority, was the gradual concentration of power in the governments of the regional kingdoms. It took place at the expense both of the universal authorities which stood above the kingdom and of the internal powers which stood beneath the Crown; but it arose primarily from the changing character of relationships within the kingdom—from a transformation in the nature of the regional community. The older view of rule and power incorporated men's acceptance of the sway of authorities external to the community—of Pope and Emperor. This acceptance itself followed, however, from the segmentary condition of the community, a condition which involved the belief that the community and its ruler were subordinate to God and the law. We may say, indeed, that a Pope or an Emperor would have had to be invented by the European communities during their segmentary phase, to be a visible symbol of God and this law, if both had not in any case come into existence alongside them. The days of the Pope and Emperor were numbered, on the other hand, even in this limited capacity, and the older attitudes to the law were doomed, as soon as the growth of regional government began to take the communities beyond the segmentary stage.

We are tempted to add that at that point the discovery of the notion of sovereignty within the regional communities was assured. But if we recall that the kings had themselves assumed a theocratic character during the community's segmentary stage, after the fashion of the Pope and the Emperor in relation to segmentary Christendom, we shall recognize that this new way of thinking about authority was not an automatic consequence of the victory of regional monarchy over the universal authorities on the one hand and over the segmentary condition on the other. In fact it followed not merely from that victory on the part of regional government but from the particular way in which the victory was accomplished; and that in its turn was dictated by the special character of the communities within and by means of which it was achieved.

Unlike those of Islam, the separate communities of Europe had passed beyond the tribal stage—were already communities under the rule of kings—before the universalist-theocratic aims of Papacy and Empire were developed. Unlike the Islamic communities—and unlike those of ancient and medieval China, another area which recognized the largely nominal rule of a single but largely theocratic authority and which persisted as a single but highly segmentary society into recent times—they had accordingly opposed to the pretensions of the universalist authorities not only, as we have seen, a formidable *de facto* obstacle but also, in one important direction, a different attitude to political authority.

One of the differences between authority and mere power is that a distinction is always drawn in the case of authority between the person and the office of its wielder. The universalist theocratic authorities in medieval Christendom did not escape the implications of this distinction. Even the Pope was only the bearer for the time being of a permanent dignity; even the Emperor was only the representative of the Empire. If only for this reason Emperor and Pope were always confronted by the problem that they needed each other. According to papal theory the individual Pope ruled solely by inheritance from St. Peter—once he had been appointed by the Emperor, as was the case at first, or, later, had been elevated to his office by the electoral procedures of the Church. According to papal theory, again, the Emperor ruled solely by virtue of his coronation by the Pope (with some uncertainty as to by what process he had been selected for coronation); and according to imperial theory he ruled either directly as the agent of God (with the same uncertainty as to how he had been selected) or directly as the successor of the Roman Emperors (with a vestigial dependence on the people of the city of Rome). Since the title *Rex Dei Gratia* similarly sanctified the office of monarch, rather than the individual ruler, the king in the community also needed an additional specific title to rule even after he had become, from Merovingian times, with the conquest of all secular life by the Christian religion, the guardian of his community as the representative of God. And in most of the kingdoms of Europe throughout the Middle Ages the king's specific title to rule, unlike that of Pope and Emperor in Christendom but like that of the Byzantine Emperor, was obtained from the consent of the community itself in the form of its election of the monarch. From Frankish times election had ceased to be the actual making of a king in the sense of conferring upon an individual the powers which belonged to the community. From that time it had usually involved only the formal recognition as suitable to rule of the member of the throneworthy family who had succeeded to the throne. Yet the doctrine that the ruler was instituted by and for the sake of the people—an older doctrine than the opposite idea of kingship as a divinely instituted authority—was repeatedly renewed in the "recognition" that formed part of the coronation services.

Nor was the principle that the ruler governed as the representative of the community, with the community's consent, asserted only at the accessions of new kings. Pope and Emperor made no promise on succeeding to their offices. The king, on the other hand, remained the protector of the law of the community even after he had become the vicar of God; and in his coronation oath, from the ninth century onwards, he bound himself not to transgress that law—to govern the kingdom *secundum justiciam patrum tuorum*; to uphold its *justas leges et consuetudines*. Thereafter, though he became, by his development of royal law, part of the machinery for amending the community's law, he remained bound to the people in the sense that the royal law could not change the law of the folk without popular consent. In theory only one thing could determine whether his acts and legislation were in harmony with that law or had that consent—the community's sense of justice. For the conviction was deep-rooted that the individual had the right, even the duty, to resist; that what was owed to the king was fealty, not unconditional obedience; that only a loyal king could have loyal subjects. In the absence of precise legal procedures, effective channels of political action and organized sanctions against non-observance—and in the absence, consequently, of any notion of contract between the king and the people—this theory was not easy to put into practice. As it was always difficult to distinguish insurrection from the subject's resort to his right, so it was normally accepted that the ruler had imposed his duty upon himself— as it was normally presumed that his acts were undertaken, his edicts issued, with the community's assent. The ruler was absolute by modern standards in that, since it was unquestioned that he alone had legislative capacity, it rested entirely with him whether he took this assent for granted or sought it by forms of advice or obtained it through the judgement of a court. But the principle remained; a monarch who in the judgement of the community transgressed the law of the community *ipso facto* forfeited his right to rule, deposed himself.

As applied at the accession of a new king, these principles were weakened during the medieval centuries, first by the theocratic trend and then, much later, by a growth in the power and organization of the monarchies. The person and position of the king were enhanced—were given a transcendental character, indeed—by the development of royal consecration after the seventh century. After the thirteenth century, as a result of the elaboration at last of laws of hereditary succession in place of the older kin-right of all members of a royal family to compete for rule, the elective principle, which had hitherto remained as prominent as consecration at the succession of a king, was further, if only very slowly, curtailed.

The Emperorship was an exception in this last respect. In special circumstances—on account of the hostility of the Papacy, which preferred that the Emperor should depend on papal coronation rather than on hereditary succession; on account of the ambitions of the German princes against the Emperor, which joined forces with the hostility of the Pope; and also on account of the fact that when they fell back on classical Roman precedents in their defence against the Pope's claims the Emperors adopted for their model a structure of power which had known no kin-right, but only election—the Emperor gradually became elective after the end of the eleventh century. Even in this case, however, there was a revival of family right from the fourteenth century. From that time the imperial succession was regulated by arrangements which combined the hereditary rights of the Habsburg family with the rights of a college of electoral princes.

In the case of the territorial monarchies there were other exceptions. The German principalities failed to establish the principle of primogeniture until a considerably later date—it was not established in Wurtemberg until the end of the fifteenth century, in Bavaria until the early sixteenth century, in Brandenburg until 1599, in the Rhine Palatinate until the Treaty of Westphalia of 1648, while in other principalities it had to be introduced by legislation at even later dates. This was because the princes continued to regard their principalities as their patrimonies, because younger brothers maintained an undisputed claim to a part of the family inheritance and also because the practice of partition favoured the territorial expansion of the princely dynasty as a whole. On the opposite side of the coin the smaller German principalities failed to establish primogeniture at all, and dissolved into *Kleinstaaterei* for that reason. Further to the east the principle proved equally impossible to introduce, so that in Poland, for example, the monarchy remained elective until its final collapse in the eighteenth century. Even in the most advanced kingdoms of Western Europe it was in practice rather than in principle that hereditary succession was first assured. The monarchy in France was the earliest to become definitely hereditary; but until the end of the *ancien régime* a special act of all the community was needed on every occasion of the recognition of the son's right to succeed, and primogeniture was not accepted in principle until 1791. In England as late as the reign of Henry VII at the beginning of the sixteenth century it still remained a question for discussion whether the King should be succeeded by a young heir or by an older man. But at least in these more advanced communities, if only as a matter of usual practice, election sank in significance with the slow victory of hereditary succession after the thirteenth century. From that date legitimism was increasingly blended with theocracy in the cause of the Crown; and with such success that by the sixteenth century, apart from a much reduced and highly formalized election ceremony in the coronation proceedings, there was little to remind a king that the original validation of his accession had been the will of the People.

Even so, the principle of consent at the accession of a new king was preserved to this extent; and in addition—and what is far more important—the success of the monarchies in establishing a right in the individual king to succeed to the throne independently of any human agency did nothing to establish the divine, hereditary right of a king to govern absolutely or irresponsibly once he was on the throne. On the

H

contrary, that other reminder of the ruler's origin as the representative of the society in which he ruled—the principle that he needed the community's consent whenever he departed from custom and existing law—was strengthened at the same time, and in proportion, as the need for consent in the form of election at his accession was being weakened.

It was to this other principle—a principle rooted in the attitudes and convictions of segmentary societies—that, as we have already seen, the segmentary forces in the communities, at a time when they too were becoming more organized and more powerful, increasingly appealed in their resistance to the growing and centralizing power of the Crowns. The humanist writers rested on the same principle, which they could now buttress with the Greek and Roman precedents, when they developed the constitutional and populist doctrines which they opposed not only to the theocratic theories of Pope and Emperor but also to the theories of theocratic kings. The theocratic universal authorities used this principle, which they could buttress with the theocratic belief that ruler and community were both subject to a universal divine or natural law, in their resistance to the increasingly independent monarchies —so that after the thirteenth century it was papalists who took the lead in evolving the justification of tyrannicide, while many imperialists argued that there was on this ground a right of resistance to the regional and subordinate monarch which did not apply to the Emperor, the *Rex Romanorum*. The principle was even adopted by the monarchies themselves in their battles with the universal authorities. The doctrine which flowed from it or a similar doctrine like the Roman *lex regia*, glossed to suit royal needs, was the best defence against external theocratic claims, even as Parliament was to be the best weapon for Henry VIII in his defiance of the Pope. In their early struggles with their resisting communities, moreover, they were in practice too weak to set it aside. No king had the power, for example, to deny Marsilius's argument that the People was the legislator in the sense that the binding source of statutes derived from the consent of the community; and there was no decline in the significance in coronation ceremonies of that oath by which the king reaffirmed the limits on his authority by swearing to uphold the customs of the land and to govern in accordance with the law.

In the persistence of this principle, and in this widening recourse to it from the thirteenth century, we have one of the essential ingredients in the evolution of the sovereignty concept, even if we must add that another essential element lay in the growing power of the Crown. This concept, it has earlier been suggested on the basis of our knowledge of the nature and origins of the state, is the concept which men have applied to political power at times when state and society, having previously evolved as separate structures, have been forced to become mutually dependent in the ordering and governing of the political community. This suggestion, it may now be added—the suggestion that the theory of sovereignty is not an absolutist justification of political power but rather a "constitutional" justification of absolute political power—is supported by a further point. Whenever this theory has been emerging for the first time, in the few cases in which we can study men's minds when they have been seeking to grasp at it, to formulate it afresh as a novelty, men have begun by delivering two answers simultaneously to this question: where in the political community does superiority or supremacy lie? Some have argued that it lay with the ruler; and others have insisted that it lay with the ruled. We have seen that this was so at the time of the first formulation of the notion under the Roman Empire from the first century A.D.[1] When we turn to the next occasion on which men can be seen to be preparing themselves for this sophisticated concept—to the period after

---

[1] See above, pp. 42–4.

the thirteenth century in Europe—we can see that it was so again. For it was in the course of a struggle between the irreconcilable claims of the community and the ruler within Europe's regional political societies that the notion of sovereignty was to be formulated once again, in much the same way and by much the same process as when it was first formulated in imperial Roman times.

It was impossible, now, for the requisite struggle to arise in relation to the position of the Emperor, let alone of the Pope, in Christendom as a whole. The theocratic character of these authorities made this impossible, as did the associated fact that they were not authorities within a body politic. Not less important, the regional monarchies, which had always been interposed between those universal authorities and the regional communities of a mainly ritual Christendom, were becoming a more solid interposition than they had ever yet been. Within the regional community, on the other hand, this struggle was unavoidable once a sufficient increase had occurred in the power of the regional monarchy. For this increase, associated though it was with a growing integration of the segmentary community, was accompanied by an increase in the power and organization of other forces there; and these other forces clung to segmentary views on rulership. It was just when the monarchy was beginning to try to transform itself into an absolutist structure founded on hereditary divine right; just when it was basing its theocratic position on a new non-clerical sanctity derived from its function as the mouthpiece of natural law in the community in place of the old sacramental consecration which the universal Church was beginning to withhold from it; just when it was supplementing this new hereditary non-clerical divinity with Roman doctrines which derived its absolute authority from a permanent and irrevocable contract with the people—it was just at this time that it had to embark on its struggles with a community which clung to different doctrines and which was beginning to organize its resistance to monarchy in Parliaments and Estates. Had it been unopposed, its theories would infallibly have resulted on this altered basis in a position that was as completely theocratic, and as incompatible with the development of the idea of sovereignty, as were the absolutist claims of the medieval Pope and the medieval Emperor. It was to come close to staking out such claims, indeed, in the seventeenth century, in the days of the Stuart kings in England and of the *Roi Soleil* in France, in reaction to the extreme lengths to which the resistance of the community had by then been taken in a period when few of the communities of Western Europe had escaped civil war. This was to be the burden of the Divine Right of Kings—of "the right divine to govern wrong" —in its modern form. But because monarchy was opposed by the community there was first a delay before this battle was joined and then, as the means of solving the deadlock, there took place the formulation by thinking men of a considered statement of sovereignty.

The delay arose because the central government was not at first strong enough to ignore the beliefs of the community or to dispense with its co-operation. An actual balance of power between government and the community prolonged into the sixteenth century both the belief that the Crown shared power with authorities external to the community and the conviction that within the community not even the monarch was released from the obligation and legal duties which an external law imposed on every man. It was for this reason that the traditional conception of Christian society as being in some way a single political community was not seriously challenged until then, even though the growing secularization of thought and the increasing efficiency of secular political organization had been gradually switching the leadership of Christendom from the Pope to the Emperor for about two hundred years.

It was for the same reason that monarchical no less than "constitutional" and populist theory within the regional community stopped short of the claim to total power until the same date. And if the persistence of these older doctrines—their revitalization, indeed, in the Thomist synthesis—provides one indication of this delay, we may now add more specific evidence to the same effect. It was not until the beginning of the sixteenth century, when in any case many men continued to regard him as "the Emperor of the Christians, King of Spain, and Lord of a great part of the world, whom many and great kings served and obeyed",[1] that the French king first accused the Emperor, Charles V, of being *tyrannos*, of striving illegally for absolute universal monarchy in Europe, and that France went to war against him in defence of the rights of a national state. Charles V was the first Emperor to be guided, with regard to the different kingdoms of which he was lord, by the principle that the kingdoms had to be ruled and governed as if the ruler who kept them together were only the king of each of them. Machiavelli, again, writing at about the same time, was the first theorist to dismiss the ancient doctrine by which the ruler in a kingdom existed for the realization of the law which was superior to him and his government—the first man to deny, or at least to ignore, the prevailing belief that the political power of the state was something which, acquired by force and fraud, could be justified only if used for the superior moral purpose of raising the community above brigandage; the first man to suggest that this power was something which, if not an end in itself, at least obeyed its own rules and had its own *raison d'être*.

It is well known how fiercely, how widely and for how long this most characteristic of Machiavelli's teachings was even then resisted by the European mind into which he

[1] FRANCISCO LÓPEZ DE GOMARA, *Istoria de la Conquista de Mexico*, trans. and ed. Lesley Byrd Simpson (1964), p. 57.

introduced it. What is less frequently emphasized is the contrast between the prolonged and universal calumny it incurred and, on the other hand, men's neglect of another preoccupation that was equally central to his thought and writings—and equally a step towards the sovereignty idea. For him the problem in politics was to discover how a political society could cheat an inevitable cycle of stability and chaos that was created by the danger of corruption from within and of conquest from without. The ultimate tests of political as of religious and moral order were that of duration in time and that of success or extension in space—in relation to other societies. His ideal form of government in the condition of stability, an ideal derived from his humanist, Renaissance immersion in the classical past and from his attachment to the Italian city state of his own day, was, as he revealed in his *Discorsi*, republican and limited; in his *Prince* he was outlining the actions and the attitudes to power which he felt to be necessary and justified in times of emergency for the community. And he was reviled because he was taken to be justifying these things in the interests of the amoral ruler. What he was groping for, however, was the thesis that they were justified in the interests of the body politic which was made up of the prince and the community together.

He was writing in a place where the distinctiveness of the ruler, the separateness of ruler and community, had early become pronounced, so that he often used the new word *stado* to mean simply the prince and his immediate entourage. But he also often wrote *stado* when he meant the *patria* (native land)—the body politic in which the prince operated. For if the prince's distinctiveness had early emerged within the limited confines of the Italian city state, that organization in which the segmentation of Europe's communities had gone to the lengths of the complete political autonomy of small areas, it was also less difficult there than in broader territories

to share Aristotle's belief that a man who could live without
government was "either a beast or a god"; less difficult to
become convinced that public action affected the whole
culture of a community and all private life; less difficult to
conceive the wish which Machiavelli conceived—the wish
that the separateness of the prince and the community could
be brought to an end. This is why many pages even of his
Prince suggest that the *patria* was "the limit and the basis
of Machiavelli's moral thought"[1]—and above all the perora-
tion which looks to the future unity and stability of Italy and
which at first sight follows so oddly upon his advocacy of
amoral political behaviour on the part of the ruler. And this
is also why Guicciardini, his less notorious contemporary in
Florence, was able to penetrate even further than Machiavelli
towards the concept of the body politic. In his writings, if
only in the occasional comment, we come across sentiments
which are remarkable for the time at which they were made
—like the conclusion that all governments must be violent in
origin excepting only Republics which govern within their
own home territories.[2]

But Guicciardini was notably in advance of his time, and
Machiavelli, a thinker more anchored to his age, was unable
to proceed so far towards the notion of the body politic for
which he was so clearly searching.

He hoped that conflict between the separate interests of the
ruler and the society might be resolved. But he argued that
this should be done by freeing the ruler from customary and
moral trammels in the interests of both. If it was in the
interests of the body politic that he sought to free the ruler,
the freeing of the ruler was for him the only way in which

---

[1] R. RIDOLFI, *Machiavelli* (1963), p. 252.
[2] I am indebted for this point to the reviewer of F. Guicciardini, *Selected
Writings* (ed. and introd. by Cecil Grayson, 1965) in the *Times Literary Supplement* for 24th June, 1965.

these interests could be served—and so much so that he provided a justification of whatever "Republican imperialism" might result. The idea escaped him that his aim could be achieved only by knitting ruler and society closer together in a body politic which itself became endowed with sovereign power. And so it was that while Bodin, who had this further idea and used it to propound a theory of sovereignty, was to be a violent opponent of Machiavelli, Machiavelli himself still sought to guard by the opposite method the interests of the ruled against the anticipated misuse of rule. Having removed moral, divine and customary limits on the prince's use of power in times of emergency—having removed in particular the community's right to act in emergency against the prince—he gave the prince only such rights as he could obtain by force and cunning. As the right forms for adoption in conditions of stability he still toyed with mixed forms of state, with structures of government based on the division and separation of powers in which no power was supreme. And if even Machiavelli was content to explore these culs-de-sac it can cause no surprise that they still possessed immense attractions for men in the rest of Europe who lagged behind him in consciousness of the notion of the body politic.

His writings were being received elsewhere at a time when governments and their communities, which were less integrated than in his city states and which had long confronted each other as separate entities in an inconclusive balance of power, were at last coming to blows, to physical violence, over their inability to achieve the fusion or compromise of interests and ideas for which Machiavelli could at least see the need. It may have been on this account that, while his belief in the need for this co-operation went unheeded, his amorality doctrine was so much reviled. This latter doctrine of his was no doubt an affront to minds steeped in the older attitude—a shock, as Gierke said, to an age which remembered a grander dream; "a sword which was thrust", in Meinecke's words, "into the flank of the body politic of Western humanity, causing it to shriek and rear up".[1] But Machiavelli's contemporaries were no less familiar with amorality in political practice than men in any other age; and it is therefore not unreasonable to suppose that his freeing of the prince was chiefly castigated as being so effective and appropriate a weapon for the ruler in a battle in which men were bitterly engaged against him. For some long time now, there had been little or no controversy about forms of government—monarchy had been almost universally accepted as the only right form of state—but the advocates of the opposed doctrines of the ultimate supremacy of the ruler and the ultimate supremacy of the ruled had each been making the same claim, increasingly extreme and increasingly uncompromising, on behalf of their cause. For some long time now economic and social changes had been integrating the communities by undermining the old basis of local power and adding to the reach and the functions of the centre; but this process only added fuel to the flames of a controversy which, like that which racked the integrated Greek city states, was concerned primarily with who should have power and not as yet with the relation of the ruling power to the law. And there had recently been superimposed upon this situation the explosive process which we call the Reformation.

Until the end of the fifteenth century even the most secular of humanists had held only that the conciliar control of the Papacy belonged to the clergy, or to the clergy in combination with the lay rulers who represented their subjects even in their capacity as members of the Church. Some men now began to insist that the whole body of the faithful possessed the right not merely to control the Pope but even to exclude him entirely and decide upon their faith for themselves if that

[1] F. MEINECKE, *Machiavellism* (1957), p. 49.

seemed necessary for the salvation of the Church or the cleansing of life in this world. Ideological and sectarian divisions within each community accordingly took their place beside the existing sectional or provincial conflicts, and beside the central and widening fissure which separated the community from the state. Many of Europe's communities were now sufficiently integrated, it is true, historically, geographically and psychologically, to withstand the strain of this religious explosion—which completed, however, the long passage of the German area towards segmentation into separate and autonomous states. Uniformity in religion within the community was the main cry, accordingly, of even the most extreme of the sects—who combined it, however, both with secession, as in the move of some of them to Geneva, and with the aspiration that one day they would convert the whole world. Yet this fact only added to the bitterness of a struggle in which every sect demanded uniformity within the community on its own terms and a religious settlement of its own making; in which arguments justifying tyrannicide, based on the old popular right of resistance but sharpened now by ideological zeal, were at last put into practice in religious wars; and in which, in their turn, the advocates of the royal position at last claimed for the monarch that absolute Divine Right to govern and make law which had not belonged to him historically.

Far from approaching closer, then, to Machiavelli's and Guicciardini's consciousness of the body politic, of the state as an instrument in the hands of the ruler for use in the interests of the ruled, men in the rest of Europe were destroying such progress towards this idea as they had so far achieved. And far from acquiring greater sympathy for Machiavelli's wish to separate politics and religion, they were fighting their battles in circumstances which increased the subordination of political issues to religious conflict. Yet it was as a result of this anarchy, which contrasted with their increasing need for stability within the community, and of this passionate religious confrontation, which conflicted with their need for an advance in political thought, that they came first to perceive the desirability of this collaboration between the community and its government and then to formulate, as the basis of this collaboration or as the road towards it, the theory of sovereignty which had been beyond Machiavelli's reach—the theory which placed the ruler above the law without placing him above the people.

The first of these two steps was taken earliest in Tudor England—perhaps because England alone experienced in the sixteenth century an interlude of internal peace. This interlude, a lull between the primarily baronial or segmentary wars of the fifteenth century and the primarily religious strife of the seventeenth, resulted from men's reaction against those earlier baronial wars; from the fact, also, that a new ruling house seized the opportunity presented by the identity of its interests with those of large elements in the community to bring about as a political revolution from above the Reformation which on the Continent began as a doctrinal movement independent of or in opposition to the Crown. In these circumstances and also because in this comparatively small territory the integration of the Crown and the community had proceeded some way over a great length of time—as reflected by the boast of Sir John Fortescue in the fifteenth century that the English Crown, unlike other Crowns, was constitutional in some respects even if absolute in others—men were able to come close to practices and assumptions underlying the sovereignty theory without meeting the need to formulate the theory itself. It is this which explains, on the one hand, the fact that the Tudor attitude to government came close to developing the idea of sovereignty and, on the other, the fact that arguments about sovereignty were delayed in England until harmony had broken down and extreme positions had produced a deferred religious war in the seventeenth century.

The Tudor Crown was still judged to be subject to God and the law, to divine and customary limits, as it had been in earlier times. Because of its need for a compact with the community; because the earlier marked development of Parliament and the common law had restricted in England the reception of the Roman law which had become the common law of much of Europe; and also because a new dynasty was on the throne—a dynasty whose right to it was questioned and whose ability to ensure its hereditary descent was in doubt—the Crown resorted to the doctrine of the Divine Right of Kings only to regulate and strengthen the succession to the throne. As used by Tudor monarchs, this doctrine by which they insisted they were king by the grace of God decided who should be the King, but did not argue that the King could rule as he wished. In so far as it also buttressed the ruler by adding to his prestige, moreover, the prestige it gave was dispersed among the nobility and all constituted magistrates: it was attached to the entire social and administrative order and not to the Crown alone. For the same reasons the Crown made no attempt to escape the limits imposed upon its freedom by the customary law. Like any medieval ruler the King was king *Dei Gratia* but he derived his ordinary prerogative and his privileges from the positive law of the land, as the representative of the community; and the power he received from God was restricted to the absolute prerogative (*legibus soluta*) of dispensing with this law in the interests of equity and of emergency action for the common weal. The theory was maintained that if he wished to change the law of the land it was necessary to have the consent of the community—that the King-in-Parliament was superior to the King—and even that other medieval theory by which new law or statute could not override either the natural law and the canon law of Christendom or existing positive law still lingered until the end of the sixteenth century. Yet it is clear that within this continuing framework of older theory significant changes of practice, and even of theoretical emphasis, were now achieved.

The process underlying and permitting these changes was that the Crown became superior to the community's law, as also to the external law, by virtue of also becoming the head and agency of the community itself. It was because it expressed this idea that on the level of theory the doctrine of the supremacy of new positive law, of statute, of the King-in-Parliament, made steady headway against existing custom and law and against the natural law until, by the end of the Tudor period, it was commonly accepted that it overrode all else and could only be changed by further statute. It was for the same reason that, also on the level of theory, the Crown was able to stress the sin of resisting God's vice-regent as a means of converting the right of resistance into the doctrine of absolute obedience or at least into the limited right of merely passive disobedience to royal acts which infringed existing custom and privilege. And on the level of practice it was similarly by identifying itself with the community, using the danger from foreign threats, the uncertain succession situation and anti-papal feeling to win the loyalty of its subjects, that the Crown was able vastly to increase its dignity and power from the time when Henry VIII adopted the imported title of His Majesty and declared in the preamble to the Act in Restraint of Appeals in 1533 that "this realm of England is an Empire".

Although it became desirable, even when not necessary, to act with the consent of Parliament, as the King-in-Parliament, Parliament came to be easily amenable to control by the Crown. It was hardly doubted after the middle of the sixteenth century that it was the Crown's unquestioned right not only, as had long been the case, to follow its own discretion in

summoning or heeding this organ of counsel and in preventing
it from enacting displeasing legislation by influence or a veto
or the power to dispense individuals from its provisions, but
also to take the initiative in deciding what measures it should
enact. The Crown which had hitherto been in any case the
initiator and executor of policy was thus in practice freed from
the limits of customary laws and ways in carrying out its will,
while even in theory, although this fact made his responsibility all the more grave, he came close to being responsible
solely to God, who alone could punish abuses and infringe-
ments of the royal duty to rule well.

But if Tudor England came so close to thinking of power in
terms of sovereignty because it experienced this marked if
temporary identity of interest between government and
governed—a situation in which the "cease of majesty" came
to mean not merely the death or overthrow of the ruler but
the dissolution of a body politic comprising both the community and the state—it was this very harmony which made
an argued and considered statement of sovereignty unnecessary. The Crown indeed insisted that the kingdom was
independent, henceforth, of the Papacy. We need not doubt
that in making this claim, as the preambles to some of his
statutes reveal, Henry VIII was trying also to express that idea
of sovereignty within the body politic for which the technical
language did not yet exist. But just as he then used the formula
of empire, already well worn elsewhere by long and frequent
use against the Emperor and the Pope, so he was content in the
Act of Succession of 1534 to refer in medieval language to the
"grants of jurisdiction given by God immediately to Emperors,
kings and princes in succession to their heirs". Nor was any
other Englishmen able or impelled to discuss political power
within the state in an extended form, or in any language but
medieval language, until towards the end of the Tudor period.
For such a discussion the climate of English political thought

was no doubt ready, as is revealed by the fact that Jean Bodin's *De la république* was so eagerly studied as soon as it appeared and long before it received its first and only complete translation into English in 1606. But for the reasons we have considered the discussion was delayed until Bodin's book appeared in 1577.

Bodin's book was a direct outcome of the confusion brought about by civil and religious wars in a France which had known no peace between the conflicts arising from the dissolution of its feudalized segmentary structure and the onset of the Reformation in the form of a new kind of rebellion against the state. In the midst of this continuing chaos, in which the allied elements of feudal and Protestant disaffection pressed the right of resistance to extremes on the basis of customary and divine law, and in which supporters of royal power used Roman law and Divine Right to assert that the powers of the French Crown were absolute and unlimited, Bodin worked to find some basis of ideas on which the harmony of the political community could be restored. He was not alone in making this search amid the press of irreconcilable interests and extreme doctrines; but he alone extracted from it the theory of sovereignty which men had long been seeking and failing to express. And he succeeded by following the same track as that on which Machiavelli had embarked but also by rejecting the solution which Machiavelli had propounded.

Bodin's contemporaries in France—Gentillet, for example, whose *Discours sur les moyens de bien gouverner et maintenir en bonne paix un royaume* was published in 1576—clung to the attitudes of a medieval and segmentary society and continued to castigate Machiavelli with moral and religious platitudes. Gentillet, indeed, regretting the actual increase in monarchical power and ignoring the changes in society that were calling it forth, attributed directly to the influence of Machiavelli's amoral political principles upon the policy of the French Crown the feudal and sectarian discontents that were tearing France apart. Bodin, in contrast, agreed with Machiavelli that only the acceptance that some authority wielded central and unlimited power within the political society could bring chaos to an end. But whereas Machiavelli had sought to provide this solution by wholly freeing the activities of the Prince from external religious and internal customary limitations, and by restricting those activities to gaining and maintaining power and expansion for the community, Bodin, a harsh critic of Machiavelli's resulting amoral absolutism and *raison d'état*, set out to show that it could only be provided if the body politic were regarded as being composed of both ruler and ruled, integrated as previous beliefs in politics had failed to integrate them, and if the governing power respected legal and moral rules. His theory of sovereignty—the first systematic statement of the theme—was the direct result of this approach. It sprang from the wish to bring about this integration, as the sole logical means of bringing it about, and it derived from that wish the few essential elements which distinguished it, as a theory of sovereignty, from previous attitudes to rule.

The first of those elements was that Bodin's argument, unlike Machiavelli's, did not base the case for absolute power merely on the needs or welfare of the political society. Bodin said indeed that the recognition of such a power was essential if the political community was to escape the disharmony set up by the conflict of new developments with medieval and feudal fetters, and if it was to maintain its security and achieve its social objects. But his central point was the logical one that if the existence of such a power was necessary in the interests of the community then the character of the political community made it necessary that this power should be legally recognized as sovereignty (for which he used the word

I

souveraineté as well as old terms like *majestas* and *summa potestas*). It could not perform the tasks for which a political community required rule, there must be chaos in the community, unless it was so regarded—unless, in other words, it alone had power to declare peace and war; unless it was above the law in the sense of having the right "to give lawes unto all and everie one of its the subjects and to receive none from them"; unless it was politically indivisible and thus incapable of being shared between the wielder and the subjects. Sovereignty was "the absolute and perpetual power of a republic" and in any body politic this power must be sovereign.

Having derived the notion of sovereignty from the nature of the political community, Bodin followed its consequences to their logical conclusion. Not only was the idea of a mixed state, in the sense of shared or limited sovereignty, absurd. Even if the result was tyranny, there could be no limitations upon the sovereign power except those which existed by the sovereign's will. Again on logical grounds, as well as because he feared anarchy more than he disliked tyranny and held that the sovereign power came from God and that its exercise must be independent of the subjects' consent, Bodin insisted that misrule could constitute no right to restrain, depose or assassinate the sovereign. But just as he based the legality of sovereign power on the character of the political community, and not on the claims of *raison d'état*, so it was central to his theory that sovereignty and mere absolutism were different things. A significant element in his thesis was the emphasis he gave to the limitation which existed on the proper exercise of the sovereign power; and these were of two kinds. The first were those which arose from the sway of divine and natural law, from which in Bodin's argument the sovereign authority was in no way released. There was no human appeal against the sovereign tyrant but it remained a condition of good government, of sovereignty rightly exercised, that tyranny should be eschewed by rulers. The second were constituted by the fundamental or customary laws of the political community and by the property rights of its citizens; and it was his regard for these that led him to make that distinction which further emphasizes how markedly his theory of sovereignty advanced beyond previous doctrines of rule— the distinction between forms of body politic and forms of government.

It followed, he said, from the idea that the existence of a sovereign power was what distinguished a body politic from other forms of association that the nature of the body politic depended on where within it the sovereign power was located; and that this could be decided by simple tests. When these tests were applied, it became clear that every body politic was a monarchy or an aristocracy or a democracy: although sovereignty could not be divided, it could be possessed by one man or by a few men or by many men. But it also became clear that the sovereign authority could delegate —that, indeed, it necessarily delegated in any complex community—offices and the mere exercise of some of its powers. Thus different and even mixed forms of governments (or state) could and did operate in each type of body politic because the government (or state) and the body politic were different things. Republican Rome had been democratic as a body politic but aristocratic in its government, while contemporary Venice was a pure aristocracy—aristocratic both as to the whereabouts of sovereignty and as to the form of government—with some democratic elements in the form of government. There was room here for infinite variety; but in general each of the three types of body politic had different types of government (state) according to whether it was ruled on legitimate, despotic, or factious lines.

Bodin himself preferred the monarchical body politic which was ruled legitimately—that type in which the sovereign power resided in a king but in which the royal wielder of sovereignty would give proper recognition in the common good to the rights of his subjects and to the customary rules and basic laws of the body politic, in which accordingly there would be accepted limits on the royal power, and in which accordingly the sovereignty would be exercised through institutions which knitted the government and the community together. This was the type in which harmony was most likely to be achieved in that the monarchical ruler stood above all classes and interests. Nor was he merely arguing that these limitations ought to be observed. In the *République* as in his other work, the *Methodus*, he used history and geography to prove that only the societies of Europe had developed the necessary conditions for stable government. And in the body politics of Europe, unlike those of the ancient Egyptians, the Muscovites and the Turks, in which the power of the ruler was like that over slaves, the acceptance of these limitations was the necessary condition of stable government.

It is sometimes said that Bodin contradicted himself in thus emphasizing both the logical implications of the concept of sovereignty and these considerations that properly limited the use of sovereign power—that he formulated the doctrine of sovereignty only to obscure it at once. Nothing could be farther from the truth. If anything is clear from this study of the obstacles which delayed the modern formulation of the concept for so long, and from this analysis of the circumstances in which it was finally brought forth, it is surely that Bodin grasped it precisely because he recognized that each of these elements in the equation had been rendered essential for any new thesis by the changes which had come about in the character of the political community and in the relations between the community and its government. At a time when it had become imperative that the conflict between rulers and ruled should be terminated, he realized—and it was an impressive intellectual feat—that the conflict would be solved only if it was possible both to establish the existence of a necessarily unrestricted ruling power and to distinguish this power from an absolutism that was free to disregard all laws and regulations. He did this by founding both the legality of this power and the wisdom of observing the limitations which hedged its proper use upon the nature of the body politic as a political society comprising both ruler and ruled—and his statement of sovereignty was the necessary, the only possible, result.

It remained possible for subsequent thinkers to take his doctrine somewhat further. Bodin, in his anxiety to show the immediate need for monarchical sovereignty in the interests of order and from his conviction that political power came from God, stopped short of the notion that sovereignty inhered in the single personality of the body politic itself despite his anxiety to join ruler and ruled together. Yet this notion was implicit in his work. It remained possible for subsequent writers to obscure his doctrine by misusing monarchical sovereignty as the justification of absolutism—or by the populist arguments which they brought against this misuse. A man who constructs a thesis can never guarantee that it will not be distorted and misunderstood. But it was not for nothing that subsequent theorists would be unable to ignore the notion of sovereignty or to alter Bodin's statement of it to any significant extent—that the further history of the concept will be a history of its use and misuse in varying political conditions and not of restatements of it in different or in novel terms.

IV

THE MODERN HISTORY OF THE CONCEPT OF SOVEREIGNTY WITHIN THE COMMUNITY

WHEN the idea of sovereignty was first formulated, in ancient Rome, it conspired with the continuation of the disorder and the need for government which had produced it—and without great delay or effective resistance from the defenders of the community's rights—to establish the theoretical absolutism of the powers of the Emperor and to consolidate the actual despotism of his rule. When this concept was next formulated, in Europe towards the close of the sixteenth century, its discovery was similarly a response to social disorder and political need: arising from the chaos that was flowing from the sharpened appeal to the right of resistance to the monarch in internal political and religious struggles, it challenged the validity of that ancient right by asserting that to free the ruler from restraint was the lesser evil in the light of the pressing need for order. In contrast to the experience of the classical world, however, the subsequent modern development of the concept was to be a process in which the rights of the ruler, no less than those of the community, succumbed to the doctrine of the sovereignty of the state itself. This victory—it would be better, perhaps, to say this compromise—was not achieved without bitter conflicts between advocates of the supremacy of the ruler and advocates of the supremacy of the ruled. There was considerable delay, of varying duration in the different communities of Europe, before it was completed.

But ultimately, if only when the thesis of popular sovereignty seemed everywhere to be driving theories of ruler sovereignty from the field, it was the doctrine of state sovereignty which prevailed.

If we ask why this was so we shall find the explanation in the immense intervening development of the European political communities towards a greater complexity of relationships and needs, of beliefs and forms, than the classical world had ever attained to. Personal, paternalistic theses like ruler sovereignty could not hope to gain a permanent footing in them on this account. If we wish to understand why, even so, this thesis did not yield without struggle and delay, we must give due weight to a contrary consideration. The concept of sovereignty was rediscovered, was flung into the arena of political debate, at a time when the European communities, for all their previous development, were still at the outset of their most rapid progress towards this greater complexity— when even the most advanced among them remained encased in their medieval mould. It is this consideration which explains why men experienced immense difficulty in grasping the significance and the implications of the idea of sovereignty at all for a hundred years after Bodin had formulated it. During most of the seventeenth century that concept itself was "weakened in all its nuances and exalted in none",[1] to use Gierke's phrase, because it conflicted violently with intellectual assumptions which had been an outgrowth of medieval political and social conditions and which continued to exercise a powerful sway over all men's minds.

Two further observations may help to clarify the complicated history of the concept of sovereignty in modern times. Whether we are unravelling this for the period up to the close of the seventeenth century, while the concept was still

[1] OTTO GIERKE, *The Development of Political Theory* (Eng. trans., 1939), p. 169.

struggling for recognition, or for the period after that date, at which it may be said to have begun upon its domination of European assumptions in the field of public law, it is important to distinguish between the more intellectual and professional circles of opinion and the world of ordinary public attitudes. It is one thing to establish that the idea of sovereignty became the ruling idea in public law and in the field of legal and professional political assumptions, if only in the civilization of Europe, from the end of the seventeenth century. It would be quite another thing to believe that even in Europe the idea has been generally received since that time; for in the world of ordinary public attitudes its implications are even today but vaguely understood. And it is equally important to remember that, because the concept of sovereignty, difficult at first to grasp, was also difficult to apply in societies which were becoming complex, the problems involved in any account of its history became different in character from the time when its intellectual victory, if only in intellectual circles, had been achieved.

Up to the end of the seventeenth century the problems were those arising from the difficulty which men experienced in grasping the concept as an abstract principle. After that date the central difficulty became that of evolving the adjustments of power, the forms of government and the legal channels and procedures that were needed before men could give the concept practical expression and application by replacing the old conflict between ruler and community, and the old attitudes born of that conflict, with the new, more abstract, notion of the state. This difficulty was all the greater because of the growing complexity of the communities: their demand for freedom and their need for government were both expanding fast. Modern political theories may often have concluded otherwise, but the clash between these two simultaneous developments was becoming more and more the starting point of relevant political analysis. On account of the demand for liberty the concept of sovereignty could now evolve only in the popular direction. But even after the doctrine of popular sovereignty had been fully elaborated and had begun to drive Ruler's sovereignty from the field, it was necessary that it should come to grips with a practical dilemma—that it should itself yield to the doctrine of the sovereignty of the state—before the much needed notion of sovereignty could attain a practical form.

From Bodin to Hobbes

Of some of the communities of Europe the first of these points was so far true at the end of the sixteenth century—they had undergone so little development in the long period since the collapse of the classical world—that the issue of sovereignty remained largely irrelevant, and little discussed on any level, for a long time after Bodin had formulated it. In Russia and much of Eastern Europe, to take an extreme illustration, the progress of societies and economies was gravely retarded as compared with those of Western Europe. The kinship group was still the basic social and political unit almost down to recent times. The conflict between the kinship group and the princely ruler for ownership of the land was not solved by the distinction between public and private law, and between public authority and land ownership, until the eighteenth century. Even in the eighteenth century the class of noble landowners were beginning to free themselves from their earlier formal obligations to the state. In these conditions political conflicts were to be fought with medieval methods, and to revolve around more primitive concepts than sovereignty, until well into the nineteenth century. And even if Western Europe stood in sharp contrast to Eastern Europe in this respect, so that there the concept of sovereignty was a live issue from the beginning of the seventeenth century, it is still the case that for most of that century the communities remained too backward or too disturbed for even advanced thinkers to be able to grasp its full implications.

There was one main reflection of the continuation even there of medieval conditions. Men retained the almost universal belief that the political society had been instituted in obedience to God's will and to immutable natural law in a process which had left the Ruler on the one hand and the People on the other with separate and inextinguishable personalities and rights. They had made little advance as yet from this fundamental conviction of the Middle Ages towards the conception of the visible Ruler as the personification of the body politic or towards the conception of the People as being something more than a mere collection of individuals. Towards the conception of the body politic as a single personality, in which both Ruler and People were absorbed, men had made no advance at all. And in these conditions, as reflected in the prevalence of this outlook, it was not only the case that even writers and thinkers found it difficult to grasp the notion of sovereignty. In so far as they did receive it, its first effect was to intensify their belief in this dualism which it was its fundamental aim, and its ultimate achievement, to cover up.

In the long history of quarrels about ultimate authority since the twelfth century, as a result of this insistence that there was a division between a community and its government, the main issue had been its whereabouts, not its quality or its relation to law. By the fifteenth century classical ideas about the political society had at last been firmly associated with the territorial community, and the obstacle presented by the universal authorities to clear thinking about political power had begun to disappear. By the same date the dualistic attitude had been adjusted to the fact of and the necessity for govern-

ment, and to the increasing integration of the territorial
community, by the growth of representation of the People
in an assembly and the widespread acceptance of the notion
that the relations between the community and its Ruler were
governed by a contract of rulership in which the original
powers of the People had been transferred to the Ruler. But
the main issue had remained unchanged. Men now argued
whether as a result of the contract the transfer of these powers
had been an irrevocable alienation or a mere concession which
could be withdrawn; and as a result of the improving organization of Parliaments and Estates and of the spread of the
contract notion they argued even more fiercely than before.
And the result was the same when Bodin, grappling at last
with the relation of authority to law, based his statement of
sovereignty on the alienation version of the contract. His
assertion that there must exist a power that was superior to
positive law was so far a logical deduction from the increasing
need for integration between government and society that
once it had been made it could not fail to be taken up. But it
followed from the framework of existing assumptions that,
in so far as it was taken up, its first effect was to heighten
existing quarrels.

As older notions of authority as being merely superior
power were slowly replaced by the conviction that sovereignty
was the essential attribute of political authority—that sovereign
authority was the kind of authority which the political society,
alone within a range of different associations, could possess;
that, since this kind of authority regulated the relations
between the chief power in the political society to all and
everything within it, it was the sole authority which the
political society needed to possess—it became more important
than before for defenders of the power of the Crown, of the
rights of the community and of the supremacy of the Church
to insist that final authority rested where they had long claimed

that it should rest. Even if most of the opponents of growing monarchical power ignored Bodin's conclusions, the most extreme or the most percipient among them turned to these conclusions as an additional weapon in defence of the ancient argument of segmentary communities that there must be an area within which the law was immune from the caprice of the ruler and the rights of the community and the Church were protected against the inroads of the state. Many of the advocates of monarchy continued to rely solely on its theocratic justification. But at least the more intelligent among them used Bodin's idea to strengthen the Divine Right of Kings—to argue that the sovereign nature of government authority was further proof that it could be held only by a monarch who could be subject only to God.

This tendency may be illustrated on the one side by the work of Althusius, the German Calvinist who took over Bodin's language in 1603 in an attempt to strengthen the views of the Protestant *Monarchomachi* of the sixteenth century—of those men like Buchanan, Poynet, Languet, Boucher, Hotman, Calvin, Cartwright and Knox who, chiefly in France, had derived from ancient theories of popular rights a revolutionary right of active resistance to rulers who violated their contract. It was he who first applied to popular rights the precise concept of sovereignty which Bodin had formulated in the interests of the authority of the centre; and it was he who first based the absolute inalienability of the sovereignty of the People, the indestructibility of the underlying contract with the Ruler and the right to resist the Ruler, on a clear distinction between the contract of rulership, which the People made with the Ruler, and the social contract—which had brought the People itself into being. But just as Bodin had said that the sovereign power must belong exclusively to the Ruler, so Althusius insisted that this *majestas* must belong exclusively to the People—that alongside the *majestas* of the

People there could be no *majestas* in the Ruler. Against this sharpened contract argument, on the other hand, some advocates of royal power naturally used the concept of sovereignty to strengthen the older theocratic defence of the authority of the state. In the course of the seventeenth century the ancient doctrine of the Divine Right of Kings had already been given a new emphasis by the outbreak of the Reformation and the redoubled efforts of monarchs to escape the controls of Pope and Church. Because these movements had produced a revolutionary situation in which men's loyalties were divided, the doctrine had begun to stress not only the will of God in making the king, and not only the king's duty to govern well, but also the subjects' duty of obedience and non-resistance to the Crown. From the beginning of the seventeenth century, under the influence of Bodin's heightened interpretation of the character of supreme power and from the wish to deny the notion of contract altogether, the doctrine received a final elaboration. Convinced that monarchy was now, in Filmer's words, being "crucified between two thieves, the Pope and the People",[1] its adherents at last added to the argument that the king could be responsible to God alone, so that his power was irremovable by human agency, the argument that this power could be held only by the monarch to whom it had descended by primogeniture in the male line. The Tudors had said only that the king appointed by God was he who happened to be recognized by the community. James I insisted that God's choice was announced by birth. Filmer supported with biblical analogy and primitive patriarchalist sociology the propositions that: "(i) there is no form of government but monarchy only, (ii) there is no monarchy but paternal, (iii) there is no paternal monarchy, but absolute or arbitrary, (iv) there is no such thing as aristocracy or democracy, (v) there is no such form of government as tyranny, (vi) the

[1] *Filmer's Patriarcha and other Political Works* (ed. P. LASLETT, 1949), pp. 277–8.

People are not born free by nature".[1] In relation to the ordinary and absolute prerogative of the Crown, which men in Tudor times had regarded as being each competent in its own sphere, both insisted that the absolute must control the ordinary. And in communities where this division and other ingredients of a mixed constitution were less developed than in England but where internal conflict was also endemic if less acute, this most absolutist form of the Divine Right thesis was no less widely propagated, as by Horn in Germany and Bossuet and Fénelon in France.

One consequence, then, of the persistence of the dualistic outlook was that men were driven under the influence of the idea of sovereignty to seek the unity which they increasingly needed and desired, and of which the idea of sovereignty was itself a symbol, by claiming that political power was vested exclusively in one or the other separate factors in the dualism, in the People or in the Ruler. It could not be overlooked, however, even at the time, that these extreme positions involved internal contradictions. Althusius had pointed out the conflict involved in those centralist theories of sovereignty which, like Bodin's, argued both that sovereignty was inalienable and that the ruler's sovereignty derived from the original sovereignty of the People. It was no doubt in order to avoid this dilemma that the advocates of the Divine Right of Kings either made no use of the idea of sovereignty or else denied the contract basis which Bodin had allowed it. But in proportion as they did seek to combine the idea of sovereignty with pure theocracy, they were forced to emphasize those ethical limits on the use of power that followed from the divine and fundamental natural law, that had long been the bastion of the community's rights and that accorded ill with the attempt to use sovereignty in support of absolutist claims. On the other hand, Althusius himself had not only stressed

[1] ibid., p. 229.

that these ethical limits applied even to the sovereignty of the People as Bodin had stressed that they applied even to that of the Ruler. He had also admitted that the People's sovereignty was limited even by positive law; and in particular he had been forced to grant that the Ruler retained inalienable rights if only within the area of his mandate. His followers similarly found that so long as they insisted that the origin of government lay in a contract with the Ruler they had to make this concession. They might limit the Ruler ever so rigorously but they could not escape the logic of their own contractual argument—the recognition that the Ruler remained the bearer of a separate power confronting the People from without. And so prominent were these contradictions, so irreconcilable, at the same time, the opposing extreme theories, and so pressing, on the other hand, the wish and the need for reconciliation in the light of the actual development of the communities, that next to Divine Right absolutism, which either ignored or distorted the sovereignty thesis, the most characteristic doctrines of the age were those which adulterated that thesis in the search for compromise.

It is true that it was not for these reasons alone that a whole range of arguments was now developed which sought to stabilize the situation by dividing, multiplying or limiting the sovereign power—by adopting attitudes to sovereignty which Bodin, like Althusius after him, had dismissed as self-contradictory. Suarez, for example, writing soon after Althusius, propounded a theory of limited or partial sovereignty from the wish to preserve the superiority of the Church over the purely secular state. As Althusius had developed the views of the *Monarchomachi*, his work continued that of the Counter-Reformation writers who had long been arguing for a secular conception of the political society in order to emphasize the subordination of the lay power to the Church, whose claims they had upheld, in contrast, in extreme theocratic terms. He taught that the Pope alone held his authority direct from God and that the lay Ruler held it from the community by a transfer of the sovereignty of the People. He so far agreed with Bodin that he accepted that this sovereignty had been alienated permanently to the Ruler. He emphasized the difference between lay and papal power by insisting with Althusius that the Ruler always remained limited by positive law and the permanent rights of the People. But he departed from the central thesis of both of these predecessors by allowing that the People could establish a limited sovereign authority in the Ruler by reserving some of their rights at the time of the transfer of power to him.

In much the same way, it was because of the problem created by the previous history and the continued existence of the Empire that theories of limited sovereignty or of double majesty were prevalent in the German area, where they also acquired a special character on account of the relative backwardness of these territories. In Germany all these theories accepted that there was a double sovereignty in the political society, that of the Ruler and that of the People. But some of them further divided the ruler sovereignty between the Emperor and the territorial princes because they regarded the Empire as a special type of political society, while others reserved this sovereignty for the Emperor alone on the grounds that the Empire was the political society and that the territorial principalities were not true states. Most of them admitted the separate sovereignty of the People. But in compensation for that stream of thought which denied the princes a share in the Emperor's sovereignty there was another stream of thought which furthered their territorial absolutism by insisting that the powers of the princes derived originally from the populace of the Empire, as represented in the Diet, and not from the right of the population of the princely territory. To deepen the confusion, the German theories came to grips with the implications of sovereignty to so small an extent that they all designated both the sovereignty of the Ruler and the sovereignty of the People as an absolute power; and it was a reflection of the continuation in this area of essentially medieval conditions that they all assumed that the absolute sovereignty of the People remained in the populace as a whole, that it could not be represented in an assembly and that it required the unanimous agreement of all active citizens to every important act and all important changes.

It comes as no surprise to find that in Germany the concept and the vocabulary of sovereignty were still much obscured. Until well into the eighteenth century, when the foreign term *Souveranetät* was perforce introduced, the German language possessed no word for the concept; not until the area felt the impact of Napoleon at the beginning of the nineteenth century did the meaning of even this word come fully to correspond to that of the French and English term.[1] Yet this accurately reflected a situation in which absolutism was being established as a result of expansion by essentially medieval monarchies— as a result of a successful fight by the princely dynasties against the archaic Empire and of a successful fight within those dynasties to replace old kinship ideas by the newer notions of primogeniture and the newer methods of territorial consolidation and bureaucratic organization—rather than of a struggle between the princes and their communities in which the issue of sovereignty could be clarified. But it becomes all the more necessary on this account to stress that until the end

---

[1] Until perhaps the middle of the eighteenth century the German language contained a word for the absolute and theocratic *plenitudo potestatis* (*Machtvollkommenheit*), a word for the power or force of government (*Staatsgewalt*), a word for the dignity of the government or the ruler (*Majestät*) and words signifying positions of superiority (*Obergewalt* and *Landeshoheit*), but no word for sovereignty. The foreign word *Souveranetät* was beginning to be introduced; but it was not until the establishment of the Rhine Confederation, in 1806, that princes who had hitherto possessed only *Landeshoheit* under the nominal sovereignty of the Emperor were granted the *plénitude de la souverainté*.

K

of the seventeenth century theories of limited sovereignty or of double sovereignty were hardly less prevalent in the most advanced communities of Western Europe.

In the Netherlands they prevailed because they loosely conformed to the actual existence of republican forms. In England they were propagated for the opposite reason to which we have already referred. The consolidation of Parliamentary procedures during the sixteenth century conspired with the approach of a long-deferred religious and civil war during the first half of the seventeenth century to induce some men to work for compromise and against the polarization of debate behind extreme positions. The theory of mixed sovereignty or mixed government—the theory by which the sovereign power of law-making belonged jointly to King, Lords and Commons—vied so successfully indeed with the Divine Right absolutism of the Crown's extreme supporters, and with the republican or Althusian insistence of men like Milton on the absolute sovereignty of the People, that it was subscribed to even by Charles I himself in 1642, and still remained the aim of the victorious Parliamentarians after they had executed the King. It was clear at the time, on the other hand, that this mixed government and similar compromise theories failed to check dissension, as they failed to avert the Civil War. And it is clear now that this was because they merely extended the dualism which it was the aim of the concept of sovereignty to overcome—merely shifted the conflict between dualism and the idea of sovereignty—by seeking to split or subdivide the rulership itself when it was in practice impossible to limit or subdivide the government power that was coming to be seen as sovereign power.

In spite of this there was no successful attempt, least of all in divided England, to wrestle with the implications of this experience. Only by Grotius, it seems, was such an attempt even made; and Grotius, as well as being unsuccessful, went unheeded. In his *De Jure Belli ac Pacis* (1625) there was a conscious effort to reconcile Bodin's precise statement of sovereignty with the prevailing dualistic conception of the political society, as in the field of international relations, as we shall see in due course, there was an attempt to reconcile acceptance of the independence of the state with the old belief in the sway of the natural law throughout Christendom. It may be said that by advancing an understanding of the body politic as a single personality he came as close to solving the problem as his retention of the prevalent notion of double sovereignty and of existing ideas of the contract would allow. His aim was to destroy the basis of extreme popular sovereignty claims, to which he was resolutely opposed. He so far accepted, on the other hand, the argument that the community had its rights, as also the argument of Althusius and Suarez that it obtained these rights from a contract of society, that he sought to do this by proposing that while the political society contained a twofold subject of supreme power—the whole collective community or body politic, on the one hand, and the ruler on the other—in the fully developed political society the body politic was fully represented by the Ruler, so that the sovereignty of the People was visible and active in the sovereignty of the Ruler alone.

It is clear what Grotius was searching for—some doctrine that would amalgamate the thesis that the original sovereignty of the People had been exclusively and permanently transferred to the Ruler, in return for the protection of government, with the thesis that government had the function and the duty to protect. It is equally clear that he did not succeed in this search—that ultimately these two theses remained distinct in his thought. For on the one hand, the right of resistance against the Ruler which he gave to the People was based essentially on a reserved remnant of the People's original sovereignty. On the other hand, he remained insistent that so long as it performed its proper tasks the right of the Ruler or the state could be based equally legitimately on contract or on conquest; and this was because, just as in the end his body politic reverted to being merely the People as traditionally conceived, so his conception of the state continued to be fundamentally the old idea of the Ruler with his patrimony, the rights of which he could freely dispose of except in so far as he had contracted with the People not to do so without their concurrence.

It was no doubt because of his failure to surmount these obstacles in his path that Grotius made little use of his initial ideas in the main body of his own book. For the same reason, among others, there was no early attempt by other writers to follow up Grotius's work. On the Continent, indeed, where the power of the Crowns was stabilizing absolute government on the basis of a combination of Divine Right with Bodin's thesis that sovereignty had been acquired exclusively, permanently and inalienably by the Ruler, Grotius's efforts were either ignored or else attacked as a concession to the harmful doctrine of the ultimate sovereignty of the People. In England the growth of dissension between the Crown and the country was driving opinion into the two irreconcilable camps, into that division between the defenders of the Divine Right of the Crown and the advocates of the immemorial antiquity of the system of mixed government and of the rights of Parliament, which in due course exploded in civil war. It was in England, on the other hand, in response to the disorders that followed from the Civil War and on the basis of the ideas of Bodin and Grotius, that in the middle years of the seventeenth century a few men at last achieved a further advance in the understanding of sovereignty comparable in importance to that which Bodin had made in the midst of a similar political and social breakdown in France.

In the late 1640s in the first place, in the work of a small group of historians who were frowned upon by both of the big battalions of the time and neglected by subsequent historians for another two hundred years, and then in the *Leviathan* of Thomas Hobbes (1651), who gained both immediate disapproval and permanent notoriety, there was achieved both the first clear formulation of the concept of sovereignty in the history of English political thought and a major step towards the solution of the problem which had defeated Grotius. Hobbes's immediate predecessors—men like Anthony Ascham, John Rockett and Henry Parker—deduced from the historical argument that most governments must have been based originally on conquest and usurpation, and from their reading of Machiavelli, Bodin and Grotius, two conclusions. The first was that the legitimacy of government depended not on any *a priori* views about the source of political authority but on the existence of a "mutual relation of Protection and Allegiance". Their aim, at the outset of the Interregnum, was to show that men should obey the powers that be so long as those powers performed their government function effectively. The second was that this "mutual relation" required that the supreme power of making laws for the political society must lie legally with the Ruler, whoever the Ruler might be and whatever form the rulership might take, and that as compared with this truth the contemporary disputes as to the precise location in practice of this sovereignty were of merely tactical significance. Their aim was to show that preoccupation with this tactical issue and neglect of this fundamental truth had produced the Civil War.

Hobbes raised these arguments to a higher level of theory and cut through the intellectual obstacles which had hitherto delayed—in England especially, but also elsewhere—the reception of the sovereignty concept into the body of political thought. He fixed on the dualistic attitude to the body politic, on the counterposing of Prince and People, as the weak point in existing attitudes. At one level, like advocates of ruler-sovereignty before him, he sought to destroy this dualism by eliminating every right of the People. But his originality lay in the fact that, not content with this, he used iron logic to extinguish altogether the existing conception of the personality of the People. Beginning with the self-contradiction involved in that conception—the contradiction that in a democracy the People must be superior to the People—he substituted for the right of the community, corporately conceived of, the equal rightlessness of men as individuals before the state that was their own creation. It was a misuse of language to call the multitude or the subjects the People; they were not a People without the will of the rulership. On the other hand, the People as opposed to the multitude ruled in every true political society because the authority, will and action of the Ruler was the authority, will and action of every individual. As well as extinguishing the People's separate personality Hobbes transformed the right of the Ruler by substituing for the Prince the abstract notion of the state.

The old belief in a contract of rulership or of government between the People and the Ruler was thus abandoned in Hobbes's argument. All previous theories had retained it as a result of their dualistic approach. For the advocates of popular sovereignty this dualism had left sovereignty with the People; for the advocates of double sovereignty it had made Ruler and People each the owner of one of two sovereignties; in theories of limited sovereignty it had retained for the People the ownership of rights which limited the Ruler's sovereignty. Even in the minds of some absolutists the People had retained at least a claim to the due fulfilment of the contract and thus a right to reacquire the sovereignty from the Prince in the event of his unlawful alienation or misuse of it. For Hobbes there could be only a single contract in which all individuals agreed to submit to the state but in which the state, necessarily sovereign, necessarily took no part. This remaining contract, Hobbes's covenant of every man with every man, bore some relation to the social contract which Althusius had been the first to make distinct from the rulership contract, and on which he had based the inalienability of the sovereignty of the People. But with Hobbes, who followed up Grotius's attempt to absorb the body politic of the People in the will of the Ruler, it made the populace a union of wills only for the moment in which they surrendered all will to the state; and such few rights as were retained against the state, the sole judge of what is in the public interest, were retained only by the individual, were enjoyed by all individuals equally and were restricted to the basic purpose for which individuals had originally covenanted—the preservation of their lives.

Like the abolition of the rulership contract, this view of the social contract followed logically from applying the concept of sovereignty. As no contract could be made with a sovereign, so no contract could bind a sovereign. The holder of sovereign power was a mortal god absorbing, with this one qualification about their lives, the personality, the property rights and the conscience of his subjects. This power could not be limited or divided in any mixed form of state. For Hobbes as for Bodin, if there was a contract with or a contract limiting the government this only created a different form of government—only placed the sovereignty elsewhere without, on the other hand, limiting it. In every form of state, sovereignty inexorably absorbed all public right.

Bodin had seen so far. But as Bodin had still set his sovereignty in the framework of the contract of the Ruler with the People, so he had limited it by natural and customary law; and here again Hobbes took earlier views to their logical ultimate conclusion. In his scheme the sovereignty of the state was unlimited, illimitable, irresponsible and omnipotent, was necessarily concentrated in a single centre and was armed with power. It was an axiom with him that "the law is command", so that "it were a great error to call the Laws of Nature unwritten law". One could speak of an obligation to obey the law only when it was known to be a command of the civil power, for obligation derived from sanction and not from authority. As for customary law, it might seem to have been created by the authority of long custom; but it was not the length of time for which it had endured which made it law, only the will of the sovereign power as signified by the silence of the sovereign.

After Hobbes

In these respects, as well as in establishing logical bases for these claims, Hobbes exalted the concept of sovereignty, which had laboured so hard for recognition since Bodin had first formulated it, to a point beyond which it was impossible to go. His book also marked the point in time at which the concept finally took its central place in European political thought. In a comment on his own ideas Hobbes noted "how different this Doctrine is, from the practice of the greatest part of the world." Once propounded, however, his definition of the concept of sovereignty could no longer be excluded from serious discussion of the nature and problems of political authority. Except in the special circumstances of the German area, earlier theories of double majesty or divided sovereignty were not mentioned after Hobbes's time unless it was by authoritarian writers who dismissed them as being not only deplorable but also absurd. Among later thinkers of any stature perhaps Leibniz alone, to take another indication to the same effect, attacked sovereignty as being merely an academic formulation, on the ground that all human authority is necessarily relative and conditioned, for the next two hundred years.

It was far from being the case, on the other hand, that

Hobbes's formulation of the concept became widely accepted. His ideas were the driving force behind all subsequent debate if only because they accelerated the completion of a major change from theological to rationalist premises in the approach to political issues. But they had this effect as much from being opposed as in consequence of being approved.

There were two separate grounds on which opposition to them could centre. In the first place, the old controversy about the ownership or whereabouts of the supreme power in the community became even more acute, if only in some communities, than it had been since the work of Bodin. At the time he advanced it, Hobbes's novel argument that the personality of the state itself was the necessary wielder of this power could be interpreted only to mean that the old ruler personality possessed it; the claims he made for the state could be taken to be only the old ruler right made absolute. He himself might speak of the state as an artificial man and might regard it as a matter of choice or circumstance whether it was composed of one physical ruler or of a few or of many. But in view of the undeveloped character of the organs and forms of government in his day, and given the still primitive character of the relations between government and society, his attempt to give definite expression to the abstract idea of the state forced him close to the argument that in the perfect community the personality of the People was fully merged into that of the Ruler—an argument which now became prevalent, indeed, over much of the continent of Europe, partly at least under Hobbes's influence—and led others to fear a formidable threat to the development of constitutional theory and of more flexible government forms. For there were some communities in which the increasing complexity of relationships (not to speak of the undermining, as in England, of the very basis of the old type of rule) was creating a growing demand for more flexible forms.

Even so, the problem in the more advanced communities was how to accommodate the increasingly necessary idea of sovereignty to this increasing demand that the relations within the body politic should be based on a system of law, that political authority in the body politic should be placed within a constitutional frame, that the state should become a *Reichtsstaat*. There, accordingly, as illustrated in the views of Sidney and Locke after the English Restoration, the reaction to Hobbes was not to reject the concept of sovereignty. It was to insist on retaining for the People the sovereignty which Hobbes had transferred wholly to the state, and to do this with arguments which made no advance on Althusius and Milton, but at the same time to concede that, because of the necessity for government, political authority must be divided among several independent spheres of right. These writers reserved the supreme power to the People as its inalienable right; but in the necessary delegation of this power they gave a full supremacy to the legislature and a partial supremacy to the bearer of the executive power. The People was the latent and, on the dissolution of government, the active sovereign; the legislature was the supreme organ of government so long as government endured, but could be dissolved by the People at any time; the executive power, held on trust, was supreme only so long as it operated within the legislature's law.

It is easy to conclude that these Whig views were in conflict with the logical demands of the concept of sovereignty and especially with Hobbes's argument that sovereignty must inhere in a unitary state personality. Certainly Locke was loath to discuss this concept and never used this word. But it would be nearer the mark to say that Whig doctrine constituted a belated, perhaps even a reluctant, acceptance of Bodin's distinction between forms of government and forms of state. As for its relation to the conclusions of Hobbes, the similarities are perhaps more important than the differences.

Undoubtedly an immense difference followed from the insistence that sovereignty remained with the People. It cannot be without significance, on the other hand, that in his attack on absolutism Locke made no reference to Hobbes's work but confined himself to the easy and by then unnecessary task of refuting Filmer. Hobbes's covenant by which every man submitted to the state was anathema to him; but the old belief in a contract between society and the ruler, which Hobbes had dismissed, played little part in Locke's own conception of the rulership as merely the bearer of executive power on trust. He based the creation of the body politic on the social contract rather than on this covenant of submission —thus while Hobbes had equated the resulting ruling Leviathan with the state, for Locke the society of contracting individuals, the resulting body politic and the state were loosely interchangeable terms—so that he traced the subjection of the minority to the majority back to the initial contract between individuals. For Hobbes, no less than for Locke, however, the state was derived from the individual and its powers were an aggregate of individual rights. It should not be ignored that, even when their difference as to the whereabouts of the sovereign power has been stressed, Locke's argument that government must depend on consent merged, after the flight of James II, into the Whig doctrine that consent could only be given to a government which provided adequate protection. Also, from the beginning of the eighteenth century, when the holders of Whig theories had themselves succeeded to political power, this doctrine was bracketed with that of Hobbes, as conducing to anarchy and revolution by this use of the test of utility, by this justification of obedience to the powers that be, by the dwindling defenders of indefeasible hereditary right. Conversely, it followed from Locke's insistence that government was held in trust for the

People that even for him a good Prince could not have too much prerogative, "that is, power to do good".[1]

It was the question of the legitimate scope of the state's power, however, which provided the second ground for opposition to Hobbes's thesis. On this issue, indeed, opposition to him was more widespread on the Continent, and in England more deep-set, than it ever became on the question of the ultimate whereabouts of the sovereign power. On that question, as we have indicated, controversy was contained by the nature of the problem: how to reconcile the need for the elaboration of the ideas and devices of the constitutional state with the equally pressing need for the concept of sovereignty —how to make the sovereign power itself a legal structure. In England it was acute but quickly stilled. The contemporary development of constitutional arrangements for restraining government and calling it to account, a process itself due to enforced recognition that the problem was one to be solved by the techniques of construction rather than by resort to abstract principles, was at last ending the situation in which clerical and segmentary opposition to a practically irresponsible Crown had perpetuated the dichotomy between the Prince and the People and the primitive idea of resistance to the Crown. Over much of the Continent of Europe this controversy was delayed, the problem itself deferred, by the opposite process. The consolidation of royal power in communities which were as yet less complex than the English ensured the prevalence of the doctrine that the ruler was the perfect expression of the abstract sovereign state. But when we turn to the scope of the sovereign state we confront a different problem. It was the problem of deciding how far the individual and groups other than the political society itself retained inherent or natural rights—rights which were not surrendered to political authority in the social contract or the

[1] *Second Treatise of Government*, Section 164.

covenant of submission, which were not abolished by the inclusion of their owners in the higher sovereign group, and which thus continued to stand over against the state even after the state's sovereign authority had been established. And in communities which had not yet moved far beyond the segmentary stage—if indeed, as was the case with England, they had moved beyond it at all—this problem continued to be one of fundamental importance.

In this matter Hobbes's position had been extreme. Partly from the fact that he had written in the midst of the disorder of an actual civil war, partly because of his iconoclastic impatience with existing ideas which went to the opposite extreme, but also as a result of his rigorous replacement of the natural law by command and sanction as the basis of law, he had extended the scope of the sovereign authority to the highest possible extent. He had urged indeed that the role of the sovereign, the purpose of the state, was to create a public system of moral values and legal rules out of a moral and legal vacuum. For Locke in contrast—and it was here that the difference between the two philosophies was most wide—the personal rights and the property of individuals were prior to all social and political organization. They were inviolable rights. The individual might—indeed, did—entrust them to the state or the body politic for their protection. The body politic might—indeed, did—find it necessary to establish forms of government to perform this protecting task. But it was their infringement above all which constituted the right to revolt against a government which failed to protect or respect them. We need not discuss here the suggestion that Locke derived this central argument in his philosophy from his concern for the interests of economic man or a rising middle class. If that was the case it is no less true that the argument retained close affinities with medieval ideas. It was upheld, moreover, not only by the English Whigs but also by theorists throughout the diverse communities of Europe. It became the almost universal view there after the middle of the seventeenth century that the personality of the Ruler, absorbing the personality of the People, was the personification of the state. Yet scarcely any continental writer maintained, with Hobbes, that the establishment of the state abolished the individual's legal rights.

The defenders of Divine Right in Europe usually found in Bodin's ideas sufficient confirmation of their theological proof that the ruler was identical with the state and that the People was destitute of all capacity for constitutional and positive law rights against the Ruler. But in proportion as they clung to Divine Right they stopped short of Hobbes's position by confining the sphere of the sovereign ruler within the limits set by the old divine and natural law. For Bossuet, a defender of the French monarchy, no less than for Fénelon, one of its critics, the sovereign power was bound to serve the purpose for which God had bestowed it, the happiness and fundamental rights of men. It was for this reason that, in so far as they were familiar with Hobbes's ideas, these writers were affronted, as were the protagonists of Divine Right in England, by his insistence that Leviathan could do no wrong —could pass only just laws and could commit only just acts. And this was hardly less true of those few theorists in Europe —the foremost of their age—who were both familiar with Hobbes's work and deeply influenced by it.

The Dutch jurist Huber agreed with Hobbes that in every body politic the state is vested with the sovereign power, which cannot be altered or limited by any difference in the form of government, the nature of the constitution or the method of the acquisition, and that the state was personified in the rulership. But for the community or the People he reserved, if not a continuous personality then at least continuing rights, separate from those of the Ruler, and hence he upheld a relation of obligation between the state and the community which was to be enshrined in contracts or fundamental laws. Spinoza and Pufendorf went still closer to Hobbes's position by rejecting, as he had rejected, all interpretations of the contract notion which preserved personality and inalienable rights for the People, and by adopting his thesis that the fully developed body politic arose from the covenant of submission which created the state. Unlike Hobbes, however, they too insisted that this did not logically destroy all right in the individual against the state; it was equally possible to believe that before the covenant of submission the contract of society had already constituted the People or community as a collectivity in which individuals had acquired rights. On Hobbes's foundation Spinoza developed the argument that, while he could have no rights against the sovereign, the individual had abandoned his rights to the community and not to the Ruler, and that, since without freedom man is not man, all other forms of state except those in which the relation between the community and the state was democratic were modifications of the proper form of the state. And Pufendorf, for all his authoritarian leanings, went still further. He inserted between the contract of society and the individual's submission to the state a fundamental constitutional decree creating rights which government must respect. Nor did he regard this thesis as incompatible with sovereignty—nor was it. A government's need to observe this decree involved, in his opinion, no share by the community in its power. To be sovereign was to be absolute in the sense of being the supreme and even the sole power, but not an absolutist power, in relation to the community.

These views acquired an increasing vogue from their inception in the 1660s and 1670s. In England they conspired with further constitutional development after the expulsion of the Stuarts in 1689 to consolidate the acceptance of the notion of the Parliamentary but sovereign state, no less than to still controversy on the subject of the whereabouts of the single sovereign authority. When the Tudor thesis of the supremacy of the Crown-in-Parliament was being translated into practical working form there was little need either to debate where sovereignty lay or to question the extent of its capacity. By the middle years of the eighteenth century the doctrine of the absolute sovereignty of the Crown-in-Parliament had already acquired the place it still retains as the dominant and central working assumption in British politics. In Europe, in contrast, the growing demand for the recognition of popular rights conflicted with the consolidation of monarchical forms of rule, and monarchy showed no signs of yielding to constitutionalism. And in these circumstances, as a result of this widening gap between the communities and the states, the constitutionalism which men like Pufendorf had constructed by differing with Hobbes on the legitimate scope of sovereign power combined with admiration for the English success in solving the problem of its whereabouts in the community to drive opinions on sovereignty to extremes.

On the one hand the abstract concept of the state as a moral person, and even the doctrine of sovereignty itself, were blunted and obscured when Montesquieu, like the Founding Fathers of the American Constitution after him, mistook the English principle of mixed government, based on the separation of different government powers, to be a doctrine resulting from and justifying the deliberate division of sovereignty itself among several independent owners. In the same way, Wolff and other German writers pushed Pufendorf's insistence on the rights of the individual against the state to this conclusion, by asserting that the community was free to choose how much power to devolve upon government and how much to retain. On the other hand, while established government rigidly upheld against such incursions the doctrine that the Ruler was the necessary personification of the community and the sole bearer of sovereign power, Rousseau dismissed both this authoritarian thesis and this constitutionalist undermining of the notion of sovereignty itself by reviving Hobbes's radical formulation of that notion.

There was only one essential difference between the argument of Rousseau's *Contrat social* (1756) and that of *Leviathan*. Rousseau took over every ingredient in Hobbes's statement but made it yield, not the exclusive and omnipotent sovereignty of the rulership whatever its form, but the exclusive and omnipotent sovereignty of the community or the People. Like Hobbes, he insisted on the concept of the state as a unitary personality, eliminating from the contract theory all vestige of the ancient idea that the constituted body politic accepted government via a contract with the Ruler. Like Hobbes he replaced this ruler-society contract with the demand for the total and permanent submission of each associate individual, with all his rights, to the state. Like Hobbes, he based this demand on the free consent of individuals, and justified it with the need to respect the equality of individuals: only this total submission could enable the state to perform its task of recreating in political society the liberty and equality of the state of nature which the state of nature had been unable to preserve. Like Hobbes, he insisted that the sovereignty of the state was illimitable in scope: it could do everything and it could do nothing that was wrong. But unlike Hobbes he equated the state with the body politic of the people that was formed by the social contract between associated individuals, reducing government, the rulership, to a mere commission.

Locke had gone almost as far when he had insisted that government was merely the bearer of executive power on trust for the community. But in Locke's case remnants of the belief in a contract between the community and the government had restricted the right of revolution against the government to occasions when government had betrayed its trust or failed in its proper task. For Rousseau the power to dismiss government, which was merely the non-sovereign executor of the legislative commands of the sovereign community, was permanently exercised by the community, which automatically suspended the government's commission whenever it assembled, because the unlimited sovereignty of the people could be bound by no law or constitution and could not be transferred even as to its exercise. He accordingly rejected constitutionalist notions—the division of powers and the idea of representation no less than all attempts to divide the sovereign authority itself—as absolutely as he opposed the notion that the state, which could alone possess the sovereign authority, was identical with the rulership or in any way distinct from the social body produced by the social contract.

In the light of these views we can readily agree that "with Rousseau the history of the doctrine of popular sovereignty closes".[1] This is scarcely less true of the development, within the political society, of the concept of sovereignty itself. Since Rousseau's time the doctrine of popular sovereignty has frequently been restated. But it will be found that, while Rousseau's statement of it can be modified in detail, it cannot in essence be outdone. Since the American and French Revolutions towards the end of the eighteenth century it has sooner or later come to be the prevalent doctrine, at least in all the more advanced political societies. In proportion as it has established itself, however, it will equally be found that it has not only been unable to augment Rousseau's principles but has been forced to weaken them by accommodation to the

[1] OTTO GIERKE, *The Development of Political Theory* (Eng. trans., 1939), p. 183.

facts of political organization; and this adjustment has consistently taken the form of compromise with the doctrine of Hobbes or the doctrines of Hobbes's constitutionalist and pre-Rousseau critics. Nor need we look far for the explanation. The basic fact about political organization which Rousseau ignored—which, rather, he tried in vain to destroy—and to which both Hobbes and his constitutionalist critics had granted a central importance is the ineradicable distinction between the political community and the state which is indispensable to it.

Rousseau's own failure to eliminate this fissure is patent. Reversing Hobbes's thesis, in which the state dominated the community which created it while remaining separate from it, he allowed the community to swallow up the state—and left the community with no organ capable of exercising power. For though even he recognized that some government organ was unavoidable, and expressly divested the sovereign people of the government's function of executing the laws, he expressly demoted that function to be a dependent function and government to be a non-sovereign body—and was thus forced to wrestle with the problem of extracting a fully competent unitary state personality from a collective sum of individuals by the device of "the general will" that was different from the will of the majority or the will of all. And it is because this problem, insoluble for him, has remained insoluble that subsequent attempts to create a unitary state personality composed of both the community and the state have either been essentially restatements of Hobbes's position, as was Hegel's doctrine that it was a law of history that a nation must perfect itself by evolving into an organic union with and under the state, or else have developed on the basis of constitutionalist opposition to Hobbes the thesis that this unitary personality exists theoretically over and above both the executive state and the community as something which these elements combine to create but which leaves them, practically, fundamentally distinct.

This modern trend in constitutional thought began with Kant in the 1780s. Accepting Rousseau's popular sovereignty in principle, he nevertheless insisted that the state, in principle only the agent and the representative of the sovereign general will, was in fact Hobbes's sovereign which absorbed all popular rights, including the right to rebel or disobey. But he also insisted that it followed from this contrast between the validity of popular sovereignty as a directive theorem and the practical necessity of political organization, by which the popular will can be active only in a representative assembly and sinks into impotence against the executive power, that men must leave aside the question of the origin of the state in order to concern themselves with its legal basis, and that the only legal form of state is the constitutional state. And it followed, he thought, from the problem of the constitutional state, in which the division of powers is in conflict with the freedom of the executive power, that men must take a further step. They must substitute for the theoretical sovereignty of the people and the actual sovereignty of the executive state the sovereignty of a notional state which was equivalent to the law or even to the law of reason. It is along this track that the concept of sovereignty has been developed ever since.

As the principle of popular sovereignty has come to prevail against principles justifying ruler absolutism it has everywhere been found necessary, in time, to guard against its justification of popular tyranny and its culmination in anarchy by channelling it through the forms of the constitutional state. Since the forms of the constitutional state, in particular the division of powers which expresses the abiding division between the political society and its government, have in turn threatened the collaboration between a society and its government—a collaboration which has become progressively more central to the stability of the body politic—it has usually been necessary to take a further step, at least since Bentham and Austin in England from the 1830s were driven by this problem to reiterate Hobbes's thesis that, however much the fact may be obscured by complicated constitutional and legal forms, law is the command of a discoverable, physical sovereign authority armed with power. This step was to look for some formula by which the old dualism of Ruler and People could be destroyed, could indeed be replaced by a correlation of their needs and rights, despite their continuing and unavoidable separate existence. And the only formula which has yet proved capable of encompassing this task is the concept of the sovereignty in the body politic of a state-personality which is neither the physical executive state nor the physical political community but a notional bearer of power which finds embodiment in whatever form may be appropriate in each case, in the Crown-in-Parliament, in the constitution, in the law of the land or even—since men are not nice in their use of political terms—in the sovereign People or the sovereign state somewhat vaguely conceived of.

It may be said that this is an imperfect solution of the ancient problem: where does sovereignty lie? In practice, men have everywhere preferred it to the only alternative, to the conclusion that there is no sovereign authority within the community. It may be felt that it signally fails to settle that other ancient question: what are the limits on the scope of sovereign power? Yet it is by this formula alone that, in so far as it can be answered, this question is ever settled—or, rather, it is settled by the fluctuating but ever necessary compromise between government and community from which this formula has taken its rise.

V

THE CONCEPT OF SOVEREIGNTY IN THE HISTORY OF RELATIONS BETWEEN STATES

APPLIED to the community, in the context of the internal structure of a political society, the concept of sovereignty has involved the belief that there is an absolute political power within the community. Applied to the problems which arise in the relations between political communities, its function has been to express the antithesis of this argument—the principle that internationally, over and above the collection of communities, no supreme authority exists.

In theory this is not a paradoxical outcome but a logical consequence of the nature of the sovereignty concept. The idea that there is a sovereign authority within the community carries with it—at least it leads to—the idea that this authority is one among other authorities ruling in other communities in the same sovereign way: a state which claims to be free of limit and control within its community is bound in logic to concede the same freedom to other states in theirs. We need not be surprised, then, that in the international context the theory of sovereignty has never implied more than the claim to independence—that it has only denied that there exists above the community a supreme power of the kind which, within the community, it has been its purpose to sustain. These two assertions are complementary. They are the inward and outward expressions, the obverse and reverse sides, of the same idea.

In practice, on the other hand, men in the past had to over-come great obstacles and were delayed for long ages before they could give to the concept the interpretation it logically acquires when applied in an international system. Under the Roman Empire, as also by its Byzantine successor, although the idea of internal sovereignty was fully evolved, it was never so applied. When the theory of sovereignty within the community was next formulated, in Western Europe in early modern times, the difficulty of applying it to the relations between communities proved to be almost as great as had been the difficulty of arriving at the sovereignty notion within the separate community, and its solution was to be almost equally protracted.

The basic reason for this immense delay is obvious enough. It occurred because men had to overcome immense obstacles before they could conceive of the world they inhabited as being a world composed of separate political communities. Thus the evolution of Roman legal categories leaves no doubt that the explanation of the Roman and Byzantine failure to extend the notion of sovereignty to an international frame lies in the fact that Rome developed directly from a city state into a universal empire. After the fall of Rome men still could not think of applying the concept to problems arising between states until they had recovered it in the context of the separate political community. But because of this same inability they did not recover it even in that context until the sixteenth century, after a millenium and more in which this Roman advance had been lost and forgotten in the West.

This inability now derived, however, from more complex causes than the existence of an imperial structure of rule. For all its looseness by modern standards the control which Rome had exercised far surpassed that which could be claimed by any universal authority after Rome's collapse. We may say indeed that it was settled as early as the ninth century—as

early as the failure of the Carolingian effort to resurrect the
Roman Empire and recreate the legislative power of the
Roman Emperor—that if the concept of sovereignty were
ever to reappear it would not be in relation to the universal
but non-territorial community of Christendom that it would
develop, but within the separate political societies of which
Europe was already then composed. Until the sixteenth
century, on the other hand, the idea that Europe formed a
single community in some sense—an idea that was much
strengthened when a Pope took his place alongside the
Emperor and when the ideas of Europe and Empire were
absorbed in the concept of Christendom—remained sufficiently
viable to give great ritual power to these universal authorities
and to prevent the development of the notion of sovereignty
around the separate rulerships. Until almost the same date
moreover—and this fact helps to explain why the notion of
Christendom, so weak territorially, could become so powerful
ritually—the separate rulerships ruled in territorial communities that were each as segmentary within themselves as was the
community of Christendom or the Empire of Europe as a
whole. When this second obstacle to the concept of sovereignty was thus interlocked with the first, when both were set
astride the only route along which this concept could develop,
it is not difficult to imagine the insuperable barrier which they
together constituted against its emergence.

Even after the concept had been recovered in connexion
with the separate state there was a profound intellectual
problem to be solved before it could be extended to the field
of relations between states. What was required before this
extension could be achieved was not that the medieval or
Christendom concept of the international society should be
discarded in favour of the claims of the state which had come
to be thought of as possessed of sovereign power. Although
it was perhaps naturally the first response of some men to

conclude that this was so, it was a condition of the discovery of the international version of sovereignty that the notion of Christendom should be replaced by another understanding of the international society—by one that was compatible, as that medieval understanding was not, with belief in the sovereignty of the state. It was not until towards the end of the eighteenth century that this problem was finally solved; even after that date the solution remained liable to rejection. And once again the underlying obstacle was men's inability to conceive of the world as composed of separate communities, or at least their impatience with a world that is so understood.

Rome and Byzantium

When the Emperor replaced the Republic the concept of sovereignty evolved in the city of Rome in relation to the problem of defining the basis and scope of the Emperor's internal rule. It retained only that application in its Roman form because it was subsequently extended throughout the Roman provinces in harness with the imperial idea—the idea that these provinces constituted a world in which there was only the one universal state of Rome. After the collapse of Rome the Byzantine state continued to uphold this association of empire and sovereignty in accordance with which the Emperor was the lord of lords or of all the world—was the sole sovereign in relation to a single universal law. Other states were known to exist, of course, even in the heyday of the Roman Empire; Byzantium was even less able than Rome had been to ignore their existence. But the imperial version of the sovereignty theory was not adjusted to the problems which arose from relations with them, as is illustrated by the development of Roman and Byzantine attitudes to what we today call international law.

The Romans of the Republic recognized three major types of law, the *ius civile*, the *ius gentium* and the *ius fetiale*. The *ius civile* was the law made by the citizens of Rome to govern their affairs; the *ius gentium*, closely linked with the widely received notion that there was a law of nature, was the name given to those elements or principles that seemed to be common to the various customary laws of the Mediterranean local communities which lay beyond Rome; and the *ius fetiale*, named after the fetial priests of the city, consisted of the solemn forms to which it was proper to conform when the city was conducting relations—making war and concluding treaties—with other communities. With the territorial expansion of the Republic, and even more rapidly after the Republic's replacement by the Empire, the outstanding development was one by which the *ius fetiale* fell into disuse and the *ius gentium*, while coming into greater prominence, lost even the tenuous resemblance to an international law which it had once possessed. Nor can it be doubted that this development reflected the transformation of the tribal community of the city of Rome into a universal conquest empire.

Originating at a time when the community's decision to wage war on another community had necessitated solemn warning and justification, and when a treaty was a solemn oath, the *ius fetiale*, Rome's only approximation to a body of international law, became an anachronism in the days of Rome's imperial domination of a huge territory. The Emperor Claudius in the middle of the first century A.D. revived or prolonged its use when making treaties with client kings; but even in his own day he had a reputation as an antiquarian. It was this same extension and consolidation of imperial control which altered the Roman conception of the *ius gentium*. It is sometimes said that this now replaced the *ius fetiale* as Rome's primitive international law—as a public law for use in transactions with other independent political groups—but the alteration was in the opposite direction. What had once been a collection of principles observed to be common or natural to the customary laws of various separate communities became a set of rules for private persons who were all subject to Rome but who continued to inhabit the many different customary communities which Rome controlled loosely, by the imperial method. Nor was it in this way only, as the name for the law governing the increasing flow of transactions between Roman subjects who inhabited different customary communities under Rome's sway, that the *ius gentium* became more regularized. Since the *ius civile* remained restricted to citizens of Rome, and since commercial transactions between citizens and non-citizen subjects multiplied, it was also pressed into use in these transactions. And since the *ius civile* failed to keep pace with the changing and increasing needs of a city which had become an empire, the *ius gentium* even provided the basis for that case law or magistrates' law (*ius honorarium*) which was developed to meet the needs of citizens in many fields like that of shipping to which the rigid *ius civile* did not extend.

In all these ways, while the *ius fetiale* died, the *ius gentium*, instead of remaining merely what was common to the laws of all peoples, and far from developing into a public law for use in Rome's relations with independent political groups, came to be regarded as the law applied to private persons within the single if variegated polity which Rome controlled—became, indeed, alongside the *ius civile* which was restricted to the city and its citizens, a single universal law which the Roman Empire applied in private (and largely in commercial) cases to citizen and subject alike.

If it also retained something of its old character, as being based on the general principles of the natural law that was common to all men, this is understandable: Rome as an empire was inclined to think that she governed all men and that her own universal law was closely related to the natural law. And if the Roman Empire, like Byzantium after it, subsequently made no concession from this universalist outlook—failed to develop, in other words, an international law in place of the defunct *ius fetiale*—this is understandable too. In the political practice of modern states the control which even the greatest state can exercise beyond the borders of its community is of a different order from that which it exerts within them, and the loyalties it commands among its subjects have no parallel in the sentiments which men who are not its subjects can express towards it. With the far less developed government machine of ancient times the universalist outlook was natural because these differences were far less marked. When a government controls all its territories in only a loose fashion, every area in which it has influence, even that in which it has the loosest claim to control, will be regarded as being on a level with every other such area, even that in which its control is most complete.

The Medieval Centuries

For all its looseness by modern standards, the control which Rome had exercised far surpassed that which could be claimed by any universal authority in Europe after Rome's collapse. On the other hand, while Europe's distinct communities developed under the rule of kings after the failure of the Carolingian effort to resurrect the Roman Empire and to recreate the legislative power of the Roman Emperor, the unconsolidated character of these regional communities, aided by the spread of revealed religion, gave universal authorities an immense ritual power. And this is the key to the inter-community or supra-community views of the medieval centuries, and in particular to the character which men in Europe attributed to the Roman *ius gentium* after the revival of their knowledge of and interest in the Roman texts in the twelfth century.

By that time the spread and the enormous influence of the

Christian religion, with its conviction that God was the author of the universal order, had given to the natural law the status and sanctity of divine law. It was the law which had been implanted by God in men's reason for the attainment of Christendom's earthly ends. When, therefore, on the basis of the Roman view that the natural law was one of its sources, the *ius gentium* continued to be regarded as overlapping with, or as being a branch of, the divine natural law which was binding on all men, the *ius gentium* similarly acquired increased sanctity. By that time also, however, the subject provinces of Rome in Europe had long ago evolved into distinct communities under the rule of kings, and the amalgamation of the customary laws of the Roman provinces with the laws of the barbarian tribes had produced different territorialized systems of law. Accordingly, as most men understood it by the thirteenth century, the *ius gentium* was that part of the natural law which—to an extent that had not been possible or necessary in the days of Rome—overrode positive law in the sense that it still applied to all men when account was taken of the regional political groups into which mankind had become divided as a result of the deterioration of human nature after the Fall. It was the law which applied to the various human societies (with their different positive or civil laws) into which the natural one-ness of perfect primitive society had regrettably disintegrated under the influence of the sinfulness of men.

By the thirteenth century, under the influence of classical ideas and in response to the development of the power of the state in some of the territorial kingdoms, we can see the beginnings of a division of opinion about the function of the *ius gentium* in its capacity as a law for these separate societies. While the majority of men continued to regard it as a law which imposed the strict dictates of the natural divine law upon all mankind *despite the division of men into separate kingdoms*, some few thinkers asserted now that it was a law for the kingdoms in the sense that it was that part of the natural law which took account of the coming of sin into the world—and which thus sanctioned, as expedient, practices and institutions which the natural law would not have sanctioned if men had continued in perfection. Under this second interpretation it was the law which justified action, including war, in defence of the kingdom. It was the law providing the rules, common to all peoples, which were made necessary by the existence of the separate kingdoms—the rules which applied to slavery, conquest, behaviour in war, the exchange of prisoners, military service, truce and peace negotiations and other problems involved in the relations between states.

But it is clear that on the one hand these men had grave difficulty in consistently distinguishing the *ius naturale*, the *ius gentium* and the *ius civile* when they attempted to apply these laws which they had found in the Roman texts to the different world which they now inhabited. Thus they tended to equate the whole of Roman law with the natural law and to be content with terminological statements when trying to distinguish between its different legal categories—with saying that the same rule was natural as to its origin, civil as to its application and of the *ius gentium* in so far as it was commonly observed; or that while the natural law sanctioned civil law a civil law was of the *ius gentium* if it applied to different *nationes*. And it is equally clear, on the other hand, that this early effort to give a separate existence and specific function to the *ius gentium* succumbed after the spread of Aristotle's influence in the second half of the thirteenth century, and chiefly as a result of Aquinas's synthesis of canonical with Aristotelian theories, to an opposite approach. This maintained that since the separate society was a natural human need, a product of nature and of God's approval rather than of divine disapproval of men's sin, the behaviour of the separate society—such things as slavery, conquest, war and the defence of the realm—was justified by the natural law itself and not merely by the *ius gentium* as a debased offshoot of that law.

Awkward problems were created by this effort to insist that the *ius gentium* was thus all that part of the natural law which applied to men but not both to men and animals. What was to be thought about slavery, for example, which had previously been judged to be justified by the *ius gentium* but to be forbidden by the natural law? But we may put in this way this aspect of the intellectual shift which Aquinas completed. When men who still insisted on the validity of a single divine law within a single polity also increasingly took account of the existence within that polity of separate political communities they had either to loosen the binding power of that law, so that it became merely a morality, or to relax their views as to what this binding law permitted and justified, so that it encompassed the behaviour of the separate society in a world of separate societies while continuing to regulate it.

If we ask why after the end of the thirteenth century men increasingly took the second of these courses we must begin the answer by noticing that this development in their attitude to law was closely paralleled by the change which was taking place in their political attitude to Christendom. From the twelfth century a theoretical assault was at last mounted upon those papal and imperial pretensions which the kingdoms had previously resisted or evaded only in practice. By the end of the thirteenth century the claim that the state in the kingdom was *de jure* independent of the Pope and the Emperor was being roundly asserted. But just as this claim was not yet accompanied by the argument that the state possessed or should possess a *sovereign* authority within its community, so it did not yet involve the argument that the state was independent in an international context. The claim to independence in relation to the universal authorities had two sides, as we have already seen. It was one thing to claim that the state was independent of the Emperor and the Pope within its own community. It was quite another thing to argue that it was independent of them in its relations with Christendom and Christendom's other states. And if it long remained as difficult to formulate this second argument as it was easy to advance the first, this was because of the tenacity—of the intensification, indeed—of men's belief in the unity of Christendom.

It was on this account that political and legal theories moved in the same direction after the thirteenth century. In relation to law the more men recognized the separate community, the more they equated the *ius gentium* with the natural law and modified the natural law to take account of the behaviour of the separate state. In relation to politics the more they attacked the traditional view that Europe was a single polity ruled by theocratic universal authorities, the more they felt the need to insist that Christendom was still in some sense a single community. And it was thus here that the divine natural law, which was absorbing the *ius gentium*, came to their aid.

If the Pope and the theocratic Emperor were to be dislodged, by what else, given this need, could they be replaced except by the divine natural law itself? If they were to be denied the control of Christendom's separate groups, in what other way could some control of these groups be continued—as be continued it must if Christendom was a unity—than by giving yet greater prominence to the natural law's role? In the first half of the fourteenth century William of Ockham summed up nearly a century of groping in these directions when he maintained not only that the government of the single community which comprehended all mankind was best conceived of as being an aristocracy of the individual rulers, but also that the natural law and its offshoot, the *ius gentium*, were the commands of God acting directly as the law-giver, and not merely a set of general principles which God issued for the guidance of men's reason and which might need interpretation by universal earthly powers. For him, accordingly, the *ius gentium* was the branch of the natural law governing the relations between the separate groups in Christendom and between the single Christendom and its component political groups; and in this capacity it was comparable to the law of torts of a corporation. If one of these groups was guilty of wrong behaviour it would be deprived by a formal sentence of the corporation of all men of its share in the rulership of the single world community. This might explain, he suggested, why the Jews, the Romans and the Heathen had been deprived in the past of their active rights in a rulership which had now devolved wholly upon the Christians.

When we compare these conclusions with earlier views we can see that they contained the germs of a new conception of Christendom as an international society and not as an empire. Judged by later standards, on the other hand, they involved no understanding of that international society as being composed of independent states and they advanced no theory of international sovereignty. In technical terms this was because they lacked, in Gierke's words, "any clear distinction between partnership and corporation".[1] In historical terms this deficiency is easily explained. They constituted an attempt to devise an international structure at a time when the conditions for a truly international approach to Europe and for a truly legal concept of the international system had not yet come into existence. By the fourteenth century the kingdoms of Europe had become sufficiently distinct from each other to be unavoidably recognized as such, and thus for men to wish to construct a compromise between their recognition that Christendom was divided into separate political groups and their insistence that Christendom nevertheless remained a single political society. As yet, however, apart from the fact

[1] OTTO GIERKE, *Natural Law and the Theory of Society* (1934), p. 85.

M

that the imperial concept of Christendom was far from being exhausted, the kingdoms remained so closely similar in their internal social laws and structure, and still had so little regular contact with each other as kingdoms, that it was natural enough that the basis of this compromise should have been the granting of a corporate character to the community of states, and that the natural law of this community should have remained a body of law rather than a morality. What Maitland said in relation to the concept of common ownership in land is equally true of international concepts: "legal ideas never reach very far beyond practical needs".[1] The idea of partnership between independent states and the rules of modern international law could be evolved only as and when this internal similarity and this lack of regular contact disappeared—and their disappearance was bound to be a gradual and a halting process, as was the underlying consolidation of Europe's separate communities and states.

So much was this so that this new synthesis of ideas which, however understandably, men adopted from the fourteenth century contributed powerfully to the deferment of more modern international notions by adding yet one more obstacle to the many obstacles which in any case stood in the way of the modern understanding of Europe as being composed of independent states. Its central compromise—a compromise between the recognition that Christendom was divided into separate political groups and the insistence that it still remained a single society—was a compromise based on fundamentally and increasingly incompatible ideas, but men's attachment to it remained so great that it strengthened old theories and concealed the significance of new political developments.

The main result in the first of these directions was the shoring-up of the universalist pretensions of the medieval

[1] F. W. MAITLAND, *Township and Borough* (1898), p. 27.

authorities against the many forces that were undermining them. For not only, by rejecting the theocratic basis of the powers of these authorities, did the swelling school of natural law thinkers who followed Ockham open the way for the arguments of men like Dante and his successors among the defenders of the Holy Roman Emperor—arguments which, by deserting theocracy in favour of the support they could acquire from the revival of Roman law, relegated the Pope to a purely ecclesiastical role but elevated the role of the Emperor beyond its medieval scope. In addition, for all their emphasis on the fact that Christendom was composed of separate political communities, the natural law writers themselves found it difficult to eliminate the universal authorities from their scheme of thought. Increasingly after the middle of the fourteenth century they did not merely accept that the independence of the ruler in the separate community was compatible with the rulership of the Emperor, or of the Emperor and the Pope, over the whole community of Christendom. Because they were driven to admit that the relations between the separate rulers could be regulated by the natural law only if some universal authority existed to apply and interpret it, they even insisted that these old universal authorities retained at least that judicial function. The prevailing attitude towards the Emperor and the Pope came to be that which Aquinas had first outlined in the thirteenth century. They were increasingly regarded as exercising their powers after the fashion of an international tribunal, and not as universal executive authorities, since the distinction was becoming more and more clear between the sphere of each separate community's domestic affairs and the public sphere of Christendom. But they continued to be accepted as universal supervisors who in this second sphere possessed not only judicial supremacy but also emergency executive powers —who retained, for example, the function of representing

Christendom against the infidel and the outer world and, within Christendom itself, the power to depose kings and to appoint rulers to new provinces and the role of the *princeps pacis* whose approval could alone make a war a just war. Nor was this attitude now confined to the natural law theorists. If only because more extreme universalist claims were being rendered increasingly impracticable—if only because the prospect of erecting the Pope or the Emperor into something they had never been, the executive ruler of a single European monarchy, was becoming more and more remote—imperialist and papal writers also concentrated increasingly on emphasizing that the Emperor and the Pope retained at least these international judicial and emergency functions.

As the acceptance of the authority of the Emperor and the Pope by the natural law theory was ultimately a response to the theory's need for such authority, so this modification in the claims of those who still championed the universal rulers was a response to the actual increase in the division of Europe and in the independence of its separate states. It was in this context, however, that the spread of the natural law theory had its second main effect—the effect of closing men's eyes to the significance of new political developments. The first consequence of this theory's insistence on the continuing unity of Christendom was that the universalist authorities were protected, their powers prolonged, at least in theory. The other consequence was the creation of an ever-widening gap between precept and practice in the relations between Europe's independent states. The period from the end of the thirteenth to the end of the sixteenth century was a period in which Europe's different communities were at last losing their earlier structural and legal similarity, in which the different states were entering into increasingly frequent and complex relationships, and in which the general moral norms of the *ius gentium* and the natural law were becoming more and more deficient as a legal means of regulating inter-community affairs. But the theorists in this same period were debarred by their assumptions about the *ius gentium* and Christendom from formulating, however primitively, the unmistakable international law which the situation was beginning to require— were driven indeed to ignore the political and social trends, if not even to argue that these trends must be reversed in order that the *ius gentium* might cease to be deficient and the unity of Christendom might remain unimpaired. Instead of recognizing, to take one example, the need to evolve international rules for the conduct of war, they clung to the old preoccupation with the question whether, by the test of the *ius gentium* or the natural law, a war was just.

It is sometimes suggested that this cleavage between practice and theory arose because the theorists sought to confine the relations between the Crowns in the territories, conceived as a corporation of rulers in Christendom, to the domain of private corporation law. The true source of the cleavage lay elsewhere. Not even during the earlier Middle Ages had changes in the boundaries of communities or in dynastic succession been equated with changes in the ownership of private estates, treaties with ordinary contracts, diplomatic representation with private agency, war with land-grabbing. What happened after the thirteenth century was that these issues, the public character of which was too firmly established for it to be possible to relegate them to the level of private transactions, now escaped legal classification altogether. At a time when they were increasingly requiring regulation by a body of public law, the domain of public law was already solidly occupied under the influence of the theorists by a fundamental public law—by the natural law and the *ius gentium*—which was both powerless to regulate them and itself incapable of development beyond general moral and religious precepts. It is on this account that we find that the origin of modern international legal rules lies not so much in the evolution of international theory from its medieval base as in the precedents built up through the unilateral and bilateral decisions and practices of the separate states which were ignoring theory.

But it would be wrong to conclude that the governments of the states were merely ignoring the theorists—that this cleavage between precept and practice was a cleavage between theorists and practitioners. It existed in the minds of practitioners themselves between precepts which they shared with the theorists of the day and the practice which, unlike the theorists, they were increasingly forced to adopt in consequence of the nature and development of the states. It was perhaps the most singular feature of early modern Europe that, at a time when the growing power and efficiency of some of the monarchies, no less than the growing secularization of thought, might have been undermining the belief in the unity of Christendom and the pretensions of the old theocratic authorities, this belief became more and not less powerful and those authorities received a new lease of life—and even, in the case of the Emperorship, an enhancement of prestige—in political no less than in intellectual circles. This was partly because not even the monarchies could easily shake off the weight of long tradition or easily escape the influence of contemporary but still heavily traditional thought. It was partly because the universal authorities, no less than the individual states, were improving their organizational efficiency and range of effective action. But it was also due in no small measure to the fact that at this stage in the development of the monarchies their practical needs, in relation both to their internal structure and to their external aims, inclined them to conform more than ever to an imperialist framework of thought.

This point may be illustrated by the development of the

theory of the just war. Theorists in the monarchies had argued since as early as the twelfth century that a war was just if waged in defence of the kingdom and if authorized by the prince. By the end of the thirteenth century they were asserting that the monarch had the undoubted right to authorize a just war without the need for imperial or papal approval. In practice, however, the Crowns continued to seek the approval of the Emperor and the Pope for their wars until the sixteenth century. Nor was this done for the sake of some advantage over other states, for there was no advantage to be obtained when, as was usual, both participants in a war equally easily obtained—and perhaps equally deserved—the approval of the universal authorities. The reason lay in the fact that the monarchs, who were still faced with severe resistance within their own societies, increasingly valued the assistance of these authorities as they increasingly sought to expand their power. In distinguishing their own wars, as "public" wars, from the conflicts which were still being waged independently of or even against themselves by their subjects, as also in breaking down the reluctance of their subjects to fight in "public" wars, the international approval of Pope and Emperor remained invaluable. The "just war" theory thus increasingly emphasized now that a war would be declared to be just by the universal powers only if it had been decided on by the monarch. For if a war was declared to be just, in this sense of being just, the monarchs could argue that their subjects must engage in it and that its existence legalized policies that would otherwise have been illegal—such as the levying of extraordinary taxation by the Crown, the killing of the enemy by the Crown's subjects and the declaration by the Crown that subjects who resisted or deserted it would be guilty of treason. And if a war failed to get recognition as a public war the monarchs could justify the same policies as a means of restricting or terminating it.

When so much hung on the question whether a war was just, and did so because there remained so much resistance in the societies to the hardships and the centralizing effects of just or "public" wars, it is not surprising that rulers continued to value the blessing or the denunciation that could be obtained from the Emperor or the Pope. And when their own societies remained so recalcitrant and the universal position remained so valuable it becomes easy to understand why, as the monarchies grew in power and ambition and as Europe became more closely interlocked, the strongest among the monarchies even began to covet the universal position for themselves. Up to the thirteenth century the rulers in the kingdoms had confined their rivalry with the universal powers to the denial that those powers possessed authority within the kingdoms. When they had gone beyond that position it had been only to reveal that they did not recognize the unity of Christendom at all—that in their own territories they felt themselves to be Emperors in ignorance of the existence of the Emperor in Germany and the Pope in Rome, or at least on a level with them. Their behaviour had continued to conform until then to the pattern which is characteristic of monarchies whose tribal origin and segmentary character have not been submerged by the territorialization of royal power and the integration of the community—to the pattern in which the king is the king of a people and not of a land, in which territorial titles are used only in association with sub-royal power over a portion of the people or a segment of the society, and in which the natural extension of the royal aspirations or the natural defence of the royal position against sub-royal aspirations is the claim that the monarch is not merely the ruler of all the people but also the universal lord of all peoples, a ruler of unlimited dominion, an emperor. But from the end of the thirteenth century, in parallel with that elaboration of the idea of Christendom on the theoretical level that we have already discussed, there also began to come about a change in this monarchical attitude.

It was then that at least in the strongest of the monarchies, that of France, the Crown passed beyond the rebuttal of papal claims to the aim of controlling the Papacy—an aim which was thereafter pursued with such persistence that by the beginning of the sixteenth century, before the power of the Pope was finally broken by the Reformation, the Emperor was being forced to contemplate becoming the Pope as well as Emperor as a means of forestalling the danger of total French influence over his universalist counterpart. It was from the same date that in the propaganda of Pierre Dubois and other men who worked for the French king, Philip the Fair, the idea emerged for the first time that it was more appropriate to argue that the Empire of Christendom should be transferred from the German to the French Crown than to go on insisting that the French realm was independent of, or especially privileged within, that Empire. And it is hardly an exaggeration to say that from the same date there was no French king for nearly four hundred years whose foreign policy was unaffected by the ambition to be elected to the imperial throne, to join the imperial Crown to the Crown of France. Nor was this ambition confined to France. Kings in Spain had previously claimed from time to time to be Emperor in the traditional or primitive sense—as king of kings in an Iberian peninsula which was still composed of several kingdoms. But in the second half of the thirteenth century a King of Leon and Castille also aspired at last, though without success, to the imperial title of the Holy Roman Empire itself. In the first half of the fifteenth century Sigismund, King of Hungary, plunged into intrigues in Germany from which he emerged as the Western Emperor. After Alfonso V had become King of Naples in 1453 he aspired to become not, indeed, the Holy Roman Emperor but the Emperor in Constantinople.

After the beginning of the fourteenth century, for as long

as it remained alive, the monarchs always displayed much inconsistency of thought and practice on this issue. French kings who coveted the Empire did not for that reason neglect to raise the prestige of the French Crown in rivalry with that of the Emperor. In the 1320s they first claimed to be the "most Christian" monarch; in the 1380s they appropriated for themselves the title of "Vicar of God", hitherto reserved for the Emperor. But it is still to be noted that when Francis I of France at last openly challenged the Emperor Charles V in the 1520s, in defence of the rights of the national state, his argument was not that there was no need for an Emperor. The French case was that the Emperor was abusing his proper position by seeking to convert the judicial power of the Empire into an administrative universal monarchy. And it is still the case that as recently as 1519 Francis I had himself contested the imperial election with the man who became Charles V, and that subsequent French rulers up to Louis XIV —despite his denials: he protested too much—continued to covet the imperial position or at least to strive to transfer it from the Habsburgs into the hands of one or another of France's satellite allies. Until this same turning point in the middle of the seventeenth century, indeed, the history of European politics is filled with this and other equally eloquent indications—indications which include the fact that the French imperial ambition was never pursued by force of arms and the fact that it was never fulfilled—that if the Papacy's long political decline was greatly accelerated after the onset of the Reformation, and even if the political role of the Emperor had from long before that date been restricted to the international and the diplomatic fields, the importance, the prestige, of the Emperorship was scarcely, if at all, reduced as a result of this restriction which had followed from the changing character and conception of Christendom since the beginning of the fourteenth century.

Bodin, Grotius and Vattel

When we return from the level of politics to that of thought we notice that a resounding blow had already been delivered, before the seventeenth century began, upon the uneasy compromise between Empire and kingdom, between the centralization of judicial supremacy in Christendom and the concentration of executive power in the separate monarchies, between belief in the dictates of the natural law and the need for international rules in a community of separate states, on which men's conception of Christendom had long rested. It was a blow from the effects of which that conception of Christendom and the corresponding international role of the Empire would still be sheltered for a long time, not only by the continuing imperial aspirations of some of Europe's states and by the time lag between changes in advanced thought and changes in political goals and slogans, but also by continuing confusion among thinkers. But it was a blow under which these things were doomed to crumble in the end. For it amounted to a direct challenge to the late medieval attempt to make the natural law and the *ius gentium* do duty as the international law of which Europe's states had come to stand in need. And it is perhaps unnecessary to add that it was delivered by the man who achieved the formulation of the doctrine of sovereignty within the state—as a logical consequence, indeed, of his discovery of that doctrine.

In this as in his other achievement Bodin was only responding to underlying changes in the political situation—only providing release for strains that had long been growing in the world of political and legal thought. He was repeating what some men had said since at least the thirteenth century when he declared in his *De la république* (1577) that "since the Roman Emperors were never lords of as much as a thirtieth part of the world, and since the Empire of Germany does not

form a tenth part of the territories of the Empire of Rome",
the continuing claim that the Emperor of his day was lord of
all the world was preposterous. Since the beginning of the
sixteenth century, on the basis of the much earlier rejection of
the view that the separate state was God's means of punishing
human sin in favour of the belief that it derived from God's
approval of human nature, the Protestant Gentilis and Jesuit
and Dominican writers like Vitoria and Soto had been laying
the foundation for the jurisprudential treatment of relations
within the international community by disentangling international law from ethics and theology. From at least the same
time other men, most notably Machiavelli, not content with
merely denouncing the pretensions of the Pope and the
Emperor, had been contemplating the actual facts of political
life and thinking of the state in terms of its practical utility—
in terms of *raison d'état*. But no thinker before Bodin had
succeeded in marrying these two separate trends in legal
philosophy and political science.

The legal theorists, starting from inherited notions of the
natural law, had remained unable to rid themselves of the
inherited conviction that Christendom was a single community.
As for the political writers, they also had been saddled with
a stunted theory of the state because their concentration on
the facts of political life had excluded any serious concern
with the legal basis of public power. It was in Bodin's work
that the two strands at last coalesced, producing the doctrine
of sovereignty in relation to the internal structure of the
political community and, with regard to the relations between
communities, the recognition that, because the long-established Roman division of law into *ius naturale*, *ius gentium* and
ius civile was incapable of providing a public law for the relations between independent states, there was need for a new
category of law—for international law.

His book provided a technical and hence a highly significant indication of the novelty of this second achievement. When he turned to write the section which dealt with the rights of nations he refused, the first man to do so since the thirteenth century, to regard the *ius gentium* as being a law between independent states; and he insisted—the first man to use the name since classical times—that if there had indeed been a Roman equivalent for such a law it was the *ius fetiale*.[1] His conception of the *ius gentium* and the *ius naturale* was shaped by this insight. For him, as for his predecessors, the *ius gentium* remained virtually submerged in the natural law. But it was no more than what it had originally been for the Romans— the law made up of the elements common to the civil law systems of separate communities. For him, as for his predecessors, the natural law itself, from which alone in his view the *ius gentium* obtained any binding power, continued to constitute the bounds set by God's will, through the everlasting laws of nature, to men's freedom of action; and he insisted that their international actions should be no less than their domestic actions subjected to these limits. Thus he condemned the Machiavellism which condoned treachery and breaches of treaty in interstate dealings. Even if loyalty to them threatened the existence of the state, treaties must be kept unless they had promised something iniquitous to nature; and treaties which involved such iniquity need not be kept. Good faith, an injunction of nature and of God, was essential if not only the state but also "the entire human society" was to be kept together. In Bodin's view, however, this entire human society was a society of separate—and sovereign—states; and the wish that its international dealings should conform to the natural law did not remove the need for a truly international positive law which might not coincide with the natural law at all points.

There is this further confirmation of the novelty of Bodin's

---

[1] *Six livres de la république*, Bk. 5, Chap. 6. In the Latin edition, *De Republica*, the title given to this chapter is "De Jure Feciale".

attempt to release international relations from the imperial or universalist framework—from that framework in which the *ius gentium* offshoot of the natural law had been made to do duty as the only approximation to an international law long after states had become recognized as independent entities and long after its character as a body of theological or ethical precepts had become inadequate for their needs. In this direction, in sharp contrast to the immediate and profound impact of his doctrine of sovereignty within the community, he exercised little influence either on his contemporaries or—except after a considerable delay and through the mediation of Grotius—on his successors. If we look at the subsequent development of international theory we find not merely that, as we would expect, writers of a conservative cast—in clerical circles or in the German imperial area—continued to insist till the end of the seventeenth century that separate governments had come into the world through the corruption of human nature, and thus that the Pope had a direct power over the Emperor and the kings or that the Emperor possessed the *imperium mundi*. We also find unmistakable evidence that Bodin's arguments failed for almost as long to attract most of the advanced thinkers of the time.

Bodin, perceiving the inadequacy of the old categories of law, rejected the *ius gentium* as that part of the law of nature which functioned in the international field. But it was in the half century after he had done so that the *ius gentium* embarked on its modern career as the *droit des gens*. His successors recognized the inapplicability of the *ius gentium* in the field of internal or municipal public law as a result of their further elaboration of his formulation of the concept of internal sovereignty; and so much so that from the beginning of the seventeenth century a simple division between natural and positive law was generally adopted in that field. Far from accepting, however, the inadequacy of the *ius gentium* internationally, the majority of writers, while confining it to the international field, now insisted that it must there be retained as the sole international law. Despite the growing complexity of relations between independent states they still refused to abandon what Bodin had been prepared to reject—the belief that there existed a single *societas gentium* in which the original and inextinguishable unity of mankind had survived the division of men into separate kingdoms. Despite the fact that no passage of imperial Roman law supported the belief that the *ius gentium* had obligatory force between independent communities they continued to assume without hesitation that the Romans had bequeathed to them in the shape of the *ius gentium* a system of international rules. Since they could no longer ignore the existence of the independent community— since they accepted, indeed, the notion of internal sovereignty —they recognized that the international community must be organized on republican lines. But if few serious writers, unlike some governments and unlike the compilers of plans for universal peace, any longer thought that the natural law connexion between its component kingdoms issued in a political authority exercised by the whole over its parts, few could resist the temptation still to write and think of Christendom as if it were in some sense a single structure. For most men it continued to be a system in which the majority decisions of the members were valid and in which the natural law and the *ius gentium* imposed a network of common legal rights and duties.

For all his emphasis on the fact that only the component kingdoms were true states and that they were members of a larger whole only in a special sense, this was Suarez's conception of Christendom in 1611, as it had been Vitoria's in the first half of the sixteenth century and Gentilis's in 1588. For Suarez, moreover, as for other Catholic writers, the Pope retained a universal authority which, if it was also only indirect and moral, still reduced the external freedom of the state to something less than independence, as it reduced its internal independence to something less than sovereignty. Later writers had to take more account of the actual division of Europe and of the growth of positive international rules. It is fair to say, however, that belief in this continuing society of states in which even the rules of positive international law were but an expression or an extension of a "natural" international law, a belief which we find in Felde (1664), Mevius and Leibniz (in the 1670s), Thomasius (1687), Placius (1695) and Bossuet (1709), remained the prevalent opinion until the close of the seventeenth century.

From the middle of the seventeenth century, it is true, this doctrine, which at least recognized the possibility of positive international rules, was challenged by another. Proceeding from the tendency to push to extremes Bodin's doctrine of internal sovereignty, this other school of thought, which has come to be called the Naturalist school, at last followed Bodin in denying the old belief in the original unity of mankind and the continuing *societas* of Christendom. But its members have also earned the title of "deniers of the Law of Nations" because they also denied all possibility of positive international law. Conceiving of the state of nature as an absolutely non-social state and of states as existing in this non-social condition in full liberty and equality except in so far as they were constrained by its natural rules, they regarded a secularized natural law as constituting the only possible source of international law. Much depended in this scheme of thought on men's understanding of the non-social state. It produced the conclusion of Hobbes (1652) and Spinoza (in the 1660s) that the state of nature condition between sovereign states was a condition of war by all against all in which it was impossible for any kind of international law to exist or arise. Pufendorf, on the other hand, bringing to bear a less jaundiced view of the natural state, insisted that, although there could be neither social union nor positive law between states which lived in sovereign liberty in that condition, the states must submit their behaviour to its secularized natural law—must do as they would be done by—because they lived on the same globe; and for some time after the 1650s the Naturalist doctrine came close to prevailing in this form against the traditional theological conception of the natural law as the law of a continuing *societas* of states. By the end of the seventeenth century, however, this doctrine was on the wane, as was, at last, the traditional belief in the *societas* of Christendom, and the battle had been joined between different schools of thought.

Like the final demise of the medieval view, its decline was due to its failure to absorb the new notion which attributed to the powers of the state within the individual community the quality of sovereignty. In its determination to cling to the belief in the *societas* of Christendom, the traditional view went on resisting the international implications of this notion altogether. The Naturalist view had its starting point in the acceptance of these implications. But it over-emphasized them and thus failed to refashion the notion as it must be refashioned before it can be applied in a system of international thought. Its insistence that absolute legal authority within the civil community must involve absolute legal liberty within the international community, and thus that what independent states agree upon among themselves cannot properly be regarded as law, was equivalent, indeed, in the international field to that absolutism which distorted the internal theory of sovereignty to mean that the ruler who was above the positive law must also be above all moral and political restraint. For just as the full evolution of the theory of internal sovereignty required some compromise between the ruler's superiority over the positive law and his continued subjection to ethical premises and to political limits imposed by the community, so

N

there could be no viable application of the theory of sovereignty in the international context until the notion of the sovereign power of the individual state had been reconciled in some way with the ethical premises and the practical needs of an international community of states—until the medieval or Christendom understanding of the international society had been replaced by a conception of the international society that was compatible with belief in the sovereignty of the state.

This reconciliation became a pressing problem once the new view of the international community as being something less than a single society, as lacking the government organs and the political cohesion of a civil community, had begun to be advanced by Bodin's doctrine of the sovereign power in the individual state. It depended on an understanding of the international community as nevertheless resting on something more than the merely physical contiguity of independent sovereign groups. Bodin had realized this need and had sought to meet it by crossing his demand for a positive international law based on the sovereign will of states with the retention of the divine natural law as the set of norms by which these sovereign wills should be restrained. The significance of the *De Jure Belli ac Pacis* which Grotius produced in 1625 is chiefly explained—as is the confusion of that work on the one hand and, on the other hand, the great influence it came to exercise after another twenty-five years—by the fact that unlike the Naturalist school he made a conscious attempt to erect a middle position between Bodin's ideas and the old belief in the single *societas* of Christendom.

Unlike Bodin, Grotius retained the traditional terminology —referring to the separate communities of Christendom as if they were members of a single *societas* and retaining the *ius gentium* as the name for the international law which prevailed between them. Nor was his clinging to tradition merely a matter of terminology. The main preoccupation of this

Protestant's later life was the hope of restoring the unity of Christendom's Catholic Church, in which he saw the best prospect of maintaining Christendom's peace. In the *De Jure* itself he could not suppress the old thought that the division of men into separate nations had been the first step in the degeneration of the human race. His references to the *societas* of Christendom lacked the medieval overtones which were still to be found in Suarez and in later writers; he insisted, for example, that treaties made with infidel states were no less binding than any others. But he still considered that Christian states had the duty to defend one another against the infidel and that every state in Christendom had the right, if not the duty, to inflict punishment on any Christian state which misbehaved. Reluctance to break with the past explains not only the terminology but also the lack of clarity, the prolixity and the irrelevance of the *De Jure*, its tendency to pile up quotations from past authorities for every statement, even if it also helped to obtain for the book a greater influence than Bodin's had exerted. But it is equally clear that, unlike most of his contemporaries, Grotius was also directly influenced by Bodin. For he, too, rejected the established legal categories; and like Bodin he did so in such a way as to show that he was resisting both the temptation to go on thinking of Christendom as a single super-state and the temptation to conclude as a result of this that there could be no moral and legal bonds between Europe's independent communities.

Grotius asserted a simple division of law into the unchangeable natural law and volitional or positive law, and he applied this in the international no less than in the municipal field. He further divided the positive law into divine and human positive law. He followed Bodin and his own traditional predilections in detesting the doctrine of *raison d'état* and in thus insisting that the international behaviour of states must be regulated by the natural law as well as by positive law, by regard for the unity of mankind as well as by regard for the practice and consent of independent states. In this direction, indeed, he preserved for the natural law, as for the idea of the single *societas* of Christendom, a greater authority than Bodin had allowed it. With him more than with Bodin, however, the natural law had lost the theological character which had been granted to it for so long. If he did not clearly divide it, as he divided positive law, into a divine and a human section, he nevertheless distinguished it from the positive or volitional law of God by giving it a human as well as or instead of a divine origin. He said that it would remain valid even if there were no God and that it was unchangeable even by God, even though he added that it would be against reason to believe that there were no God or that God's will was not its ultimate source. And what is still more important, after dividing positive law into divine and human positive law he again followed Bodin by asserting that the Roman and medieval versions of the *ius gentium*, by confusing the natural law and positive law, had given a binding international character to what were merely the rules of private law which were common to all the nations and which any nation was free to change unilaterally. The true *ius gentium*—the name which, unlike Bodin, he retained for the multi-lateral positive law of nations of which he so clearly felt the need—was not derived from the natural law but was that part of *human* positive law which obtained as between independent states. It was the *ius gentium voluntarium*. Its origin was to be sought in the unbroken custom and actual practice of states, its obligatory force only in the will of all nations or of many nations.

What this scheme left unsettled was the relationship between this positive law of nations and the law of nature. In the first place, Grotius left the character of the natural law itself ambiguous. Although his most frequent references made it consist of the general principles that conformed to the best elements in man, and that were arrived at by synthesis of the principal systems of existing law, we cannot be sure whether he thought it was the body of ethical but human norms of reason and principle by which behaviour ought to be restrained in a state of nature plurality of independent states; or a body of divine moral law like the divine positive law; or even, as it became for Hobbes, the body of physical laws which, expressing the bad no less than the good elements in man, operated inexorably in the state of nature. In the second place, he deepened this confusion by returning varying answers to the question whether the natural law, thus variously interpreted, was superior to the positive law. In his scheme the law of nations rightly prohibited some things permitted by the natural law—the waging of war without a declaration of war, for example; or poisoning as a means to be used in the just killing of kings—even as the natural law forbade some things still permitted by the law of nations. As often as he argued that the natural law should be called in to mitigate severities and barbarities allowed or condoned by the law of nations—as when it sanctioned the ill-treatment of slaves, the killing of hostages and the indiscriminate killing of all the subjects of an enemy in a public war, just or unjust—he advocated adhesion to the law of nations as the means of tempering excesses permitted by the natural law. But this uncertainty does not detract from the essential novelty of his book or conceal its central purpose. At the time he was writing, indeed, some confusion was an unavoidable consequence of his aim.

Bodin apart—herein lies the novelty of his work—Grotius was the first man to insist on the need for a body of positive international law, separate from the natural law and deriving from the will and practice of states; and since Bodin had not proceeded far beyond pointing out this need, the *De Jure Belli ac Pacis* was the first systematic treatise on this law. This involved Grotius in championing the validity of the positive law wherever it already existed and with whatever defects it might happen to possess. Nor need we doubt that in taking this position he was recognizing that the natural law was inadequate as a means of regulating the international conduct of sovereign states. Because sovereign states could not be bound by the natural law it was all the more essential that they should be restrained by legality—this was the drift of his thought. It was not for nothing that Pufendorf, the leading Naturalist, complained that Grotius had based all international law on the consent of states, and not for nothing that of the two schools which dominated international thought after the end of the seventeenth century, while one was the Grotian school itself, the other, in part as a result of Grotius's influence, was the Positivist school which regarded custom and treaty as the main sources of true international law.

Grotius did not think, however, that the positive law of nations was satisfactory as it stood, and still less did he assume that it could guarantee international morality. On the contrary, his central purpose was to bring about a greater coincidence between legality and justice by increasing the approximation of the positive law of nations to the natural law. If it was necessary to insist on the validity of existing positive law in order that it might be developed, it was equally necessary to insist that its development should be towards conformity with the natural law, which Grotius called "the great-grandmother" of the human positive law. He had some difficulty at this point in discovering what the natural law was, some uncertainty as to whether it possessed a binding legal or a purely moral character, some tendency to regard it as inferior to the positive law even in point of justice—some problem, in fact, in distinguishing between the two bodies of law as bodies of law. But he was at least consistent in distinguishing between legality and justice and in upholding justice when they clashed.

After reversing, for example, the arguments of his predecessors on the subject of "the just war"—after insisting, not that a just war was the only war permissible in law, but that the lawful war was the only just war; that for a war to be just there must be a legal cause for it, defence against injury or recovery of what was legally due; that there was no absolute right to war even in self-defence, but only a right to it when other states had failed in their legal duty—he asserted the duty of the subject to refuse to serve the state in an unjust or doubtfully just war. In the same way he attempted to establish by his doctrine of qualified neutrality that the neutral state had not merely the duty not to help the unjust belligerent and not to hamper the just, but also the right to assist the just belligerent.

He even extended this right to intervention against a prince in a civil war in cases when it was clear that the prince had acted illegally. Thus again, having insisted on the necessity and the validity of a positive law whose binding force derived from the will and practice of states, he sought to ground a duty to accept this binding force of treaties and promises in the justice enjoined by nature or the natural law—and this at a time when it was still widely held that the Pope had the power to release rulers from their oaths and that there could be no binding force in treaties between Christians and the infidel or between Catholics and Protestants. It is in no way surprising that to his Positivist successors Grotius's book seemed to provide rather a system of ethics as applied to states than a system of international law.

But if we give its due weight to each side of Grotius's statement we can see that this verdict was no more accurate than Pufendorf's. Although he did not succeed in integrating the two sides into a consistent body of thought, he was embarked upon the first sustained attempt, first to replace the old concept of the natural law by the distinction between morality and law, and then to establish the necessity for both morality and law in any system of international jurisprudence that was based on the existence of sovereign states. He was trying to say that in international dealings, while the sovereignty of the state must issue in a positive law which flowed from the will of the state, the sovereignty of the state must be shorn of its character of absoluteness by the subordination of the state's superiority over positive law to some other source of restraint. And whether he knew it or not—even if he was chiefly inspired by the desire to preserve the old concept of the Christian society of states—he was thus opening up the only practicable route towards the incorporation into an international context of the new concept of the sovereignty of the state.

This was not recognized at once. We have already noticed that the spread of Grotius's influence was delayed until after the middle of the seventeenth century, that even then it owed not a little to Grotius's traditional terminology, that other views than his were prevalent until that century was drawing to its close. It may now be added that these other views continued to find a following until well into the eighteenth century. Conclusions similar to Pufendorf's were to be upheld, as by Thomas Rutherford in England and J. H. G. von Justi in Prussia, as late as the 1760s. In the 1740s a group under Christian Wolff, the professor of the *ius naturale et gentium* at Halle and a friend of Leibniz, attempted even to revive and propagate the old belief in a single society or *civitas maxima* of Europe in which the separate states were citizens, subject to a real group authority. From the beginning of the eighteenth century, however, at least on the level of legal thought, the process of adjusting to the notion of sovereignty was well launched. On the one hand, both Naturalist thinking and this traditional natural law belief were yielding rapidly to either Positivist or Grotian views. On the other hand, not even the most extreme advocate of the Positivist position—neither Bynkerschoek in the first half of the eighteenth century nor any professional writer during the nineteenth century, when the tendency to Positivism much increased—now regarded the wills of sovereign states as the exclusive source of international law; while despite the growth of Positivism the Grotian position never ceased to be dominant after it had been adopted—and adapted—by Vattel in his *Le droit des gens, ou principes de la loi naturelle, appliqés à la conduite et aux affaires des nations et des souverains,* of 1758.

In this book, undertaken in the first place as a translation of Wolff's Latin work, *Ius gentium methodo scientifica pertractatum* (1749), Vattel made a direct attack on the old natural law theory which Wolff had hoped to revive—

> I differ entirely from Mr. Wolff [he said, in the last such attack that was ever to be necessary] in the foundation I lay down for that division of the law of nations which we term *voluntary*. Mr. Wolff deduces it from the idea of a sort of great republic (*civitas maxima*) set up by nature herself, of which all the nations of the world are members . . . I find the fiction of such a republic neither reasonable nor well enough established to deduce therefrom the rules of a Law of Nations at once universal in character and necessarily accepted by sovereign states. It is essential to every *civitas* that each member should yield certain of his rights to the general body, and that there should be some authority capable of giving commands, prescribing laws and compelling those who refuse to obey. Such an idea is not to be thought of as between nations. Each independent state claims to be, and actually is, independent of all the others . . . [1]

At the same time, however, he followed Grotius in attributing a legal character to the natural law no less than to positive law. And he followed the most advanced among his own non-legal

[1] EMMERICK DE VATTEL, *The Law of Nations* (Carnegie edn., Washington, 1916), p. 9a.

contemporaries when, in order to close the gap between his dismissal of the idea of the *civitas* of Europe and his retention of the natural law, he insisted that—

> Europe forms a political system in which the nations . . . are bound together by their relations and their various interests into a single body. It is no longer as in former times a heap of detached parts, each of which had but little concern for the lot of the others, [but] . . . a sort of republic, whose members—each independent but all bound together by a common interest—unite for the maintenance of order and the preservation of liberty.[1]

For these words closely followed those in which men like Montesquieu, Voltaire, Hume and Rousseau had advanced for the first time, and since as recently as the 1740s, a new conception of Europe.[2]

It was a conception in which the emphasis was no longer on the belief that the states were socially, culturally, ritually and even politically a single *societas*, as was maintained by the long-established natural law views, nor yet on the point to which the Naturalist and Positivist attacks on those views had been attracted—on the point that they were utterly independent politically even if they were morally associated and geographically contiguous. What it stressed was that they were politically separate organizations, held together by no natural bond, which had, however, been drawn together by their historical development into a single international political system that was *sui generis*—that they had become internationally a unity because of their diversity. And just as this thesis was the first expression of a modern view of the international system, so Vattel, who took it over, produced the first recognizably modern book on international law. His

---

[1] ibid., Book III, Ch. iii, Sect. 47.
[2] For a fuller treatment of this development *see* F. H. HINSLEY, *Power and the Pursuit of Peace* (1963), pp. 161-4.

Droit des gens was this indisputably, and not merely because it was the first to adopt this view of the international system. It possessed the further novel feature that, adopting this attitude, it assumed that there was need for an international law of peace as well as of war. The word "peace" might appear in the titles of their books, and they might have been shocked by the horrors of war, but Grotius and other legal writers before Vattel had still been concerned only to civilize conflict—to systematize rules for the conduct of war and for the transfer of provinces as a result of war. Vattel was equally interested in stating and systematizing the rules which should govern the relations between states in the many fields in which they must be associated in time of peace.

The Reception of the Sovereignty of the State as the Basis of International Practice

Vattel's work clearly reflected in these ways a fundamental if recent consolidation of advance on the level of international thought. It was not so obvious at the time that any comparable advance was taking place in the sphere of international practice. On the contrary, the new view of Europe was an aspiration or a vision rather than a statement of fact—a vision which, like Wolff's attempt to return to medieval concepts, was produced in reaction against the renewal, not to say the increase, of warfare in Europe after the brief period of exhaustion which followed the Utrecht settlement of 1713. Vattel's own book, again, like Voltaire's satire on war in *Candide* (1759), was produced in the midst of a further and still more extensive European conflict, the Seven Years' War. It is not surprising, then, that until that time, on a level of political thinking less technical and less sophisticated than that which has so far been discussed, men like the Abbé de Saint-Pierre continued to urge upon the world an argument which had begun to appear in modern dress during the Thirty Years'

War, in the first half of the seventeenth century, but which remained essentially medieval in its neglect of the development of the state and in its assumption that Christendom remained a single political organization. We can even understand why this argument—the argument that universal and perpetual peace could be secured only by the union of Europe's states into a single empire or federation—received on the eve of the Seven Years' War the attention of a serious modern political thinker for the first time, if also for the last, when Rousseau recapitulated the writings of Saint-Pierre in his *Extrait du projet de paix perpétuelle* of 1756.

By the middle of the eighteenth century it had come to be almost universally accepted on the level of serious thought, not only that the international society lacked the legal sanctions which served in the single state, as it lacked the single state's legislative, judicial and governmental organs and its social cohesion, but also that it was all the more necessary on that account to suppose that the sovereign will of the single state was internationally subjected to some other higher restraint. But neither political nor legal thought had yet solved the resultant problem which had already lain at the root of Grotius's confusion. Where in a world of sovereign states was that other restraint to be discovered and how, if discovered, was it to be made effective? Nor was it possible to solve this problem, given the direction which serious thought had taken since Bodin's time, unless men could close the gap between the practice of states and the conceptual requirements of this new international theory in which state sovereignty was a central principle. This gap now involved, moreover, a difficulty which had not existed in earlier times.

It is unlikely that there has ever been a time when theory and practice in international relations have not diverged. Until the end of the seventeenth century, however, the divergence had been one between primitive practices on the part of states and primitive—universalist or imperialist—precepts to which states themselves had subscribed; and it had not been acute. Until perhaps the fifteenth century, moreover, as we have already noticed, intercourse between states had been so irregular and intermittent that it had scarcely been a matter for concern. From the first half of the eighteenth century, in contrast, the gap had become one between the requirements of the body of sophisticated legal and moral thought to which theorists had been driven by the actual and notional development of the state and, on the other hand, the tendency for the international behaviour of states to remain embedded in a primitive mould despite the fact they had been drawn into complex and continuous relations with each other.

It is this dilemma which explains why projects like Saint-Pierre's continued to be advocated during the first half of the eighteenth century. It also explains why, after fading then, such projects have continued to be revived from time to time, especially in troubled times. Hence, also, the frequent lament since the eighteenth century—in some or other circles of opinion, indeed, it has been a perennial source of regret or complaint—that in a hundred or one hundred and fifty or even two hundred and fifty years the ideas of men like Grotius or Vattel have had little or no influence on the practice of states. It is because of this same dilemma, on the other hand, that since the eighteenth century there has been a persistent tendency to try to close the gap by adjusting the theoretical requirements to bring them more nearly within the reach of practice. The growth of Positivism, especially during the nineteenth century, was one result of this effort. Another was the disposition even of Grotians, beginning with Vattel, to move away from the original doctrine of Grotius in the direction of equating the natural practice of states with the principles of the natural law itself. Yet it cannot be overlooked that this last tendency was also encouraged by the achievement of some advance in the sphere of state practice which this lament has ignored. The more one studies the development of the international system, indeed, the more it becomes apparent that it is false to conclude—as it would be unreasonable to assume—that the international behaviour of states has undergone no improvement since the seventeenth century.

The gap between the needs of international legal theory and the conduct of international politics has not been eliminated since that time; it may never be permanently closed. From time to time, in deteriorating conditions, it has widened until it has become immense. But it has also been narrowed at other times by a sequence of significant, if interrupted, advances in the practice of states. And the first of these advances, and perhaps the most decisive, was accomplished between the end of the seventeenth century and the outbreak of the French Revolution, just when the replacement of the medieval by the modern outlook in the sphere of theory was finally being consolidated. For we may see that it was at that juncture in the long history of the political community, though only in Europe, that international conduct at last passed from the primitive into at least a post-primitive phase.

The primitive pattern of international conduct may be said to prevail wherever and for so long as the communities in an international system remain basically segmentary communities governed by primitive states. The central feature of this pattern is the search by the state in each of the communities for physical conflict with the other states; and, if things go reasonably well for one of the states, this search aims at the consolidation of all the communities sharing some ritual or natural unity, or which are within practicable range, into a single empire. All the main indications suggest that the European communities were of this character and in the grip of this pattern from the end of their tribal days until the eighteenth century; but they also suggest that it was during the eighteenth century—no doubt on the basis of foundations built over a long period of earlier time, yet also even now with obvious reluctance and at no great speed—that the European states began to move into a different international structure.

Sometime between 1700 and 1750 the idea of the balance of power between states, an idea which has probably been pursued instinctively throughout history as a matter of expediency and which had continued to be discussed in terms of expediency after first becoming the subject of much conscious thought from about 1600, began to be regarded by theorists as rather a principle to be upheld for its own sake, a purpose to be served by policy, an aim equivalent to what we now call co-existence between contiguous independent states. Thus whereas Sully, an early advocate of the advantages of what he called "equilibrium" between the European states, had in the 1630s seen it as being chiefly a means of maintaining the primacy of France in conditions of rapid change in Christendom, Fénelon in the opening years of the eighteenth century regarded it as the foundation of repose and security for all the states, great and small. A forthright critic of the foreign policy excesses of Louis XIV, he combined Grotius's view that the separate states of Christendom were united in submission to God and the natural law with the argument that "a holy alliance" of the princes of Christendom should pursue the policy of equilibrium or balance of power as something enjoined by the natural law itself as the safeguard against the dangerous search for universal monarchy in Europe. A generation later, for Vattel as for Voltaire, it was the historical development of Europe into a system of independent but interlocked states which had "given rise to the well-known principle of the balance of power, by which is meant an arrangement of affairs so that no state shall be in a position to have absolute mastery and dominate over the others". And what needs most to be noticed here

is that not long after, from the 1760s, this interpretation
of the idea began to be adopted also by the governments of
Europe.

From about the same time, to take another indication, the
situation in which warfare had for centuries been an almost
continuous activity, following an unbroken if fluctuating
rhythm, and one in which official and unofficial war, international and civil war, had been inextricably confused, finally
gave way to that alternation of periods of peace with periods
of war and to that virtual elimination of unofficial war which
have ever since been pronounced features in the history of
relations between the more advanced communities. It is often
overlooked that these, the Great Powers, achieved nearly
thirty years of peace before the wars following the French
Revolution, and that since that time they have experienced
forty years of nearly total peace among themselves between
1815 and 1854, forty-four years between 1871 and 1914,
twenty years between 1918 and 1939 and, from 1945 again,
another twenty years already.

No less significant, and still more relevant here, is this further
evidence that points in the same direction. The need for a
systematic body of international law had been pressing since
before Grotius's time—at least to the minds of legal theorists.
It was partly because he had met this need that Grotius had
become so great an influence, after some delay, from about
1680. But Grotius's influence had still been confined to the
world of legal theorists. It was Vattel's work which, as well as
being the first recognizably modern book on international
law, became the first such book to be used as a handbook by
Foreign Offices. It was used in this way, moreover, from soon
after its publication. The French government was referring to
it in the 1760s; by the government of the United States of
America it was venerated as being the guide, in the phrase
later used by Daniel Webster, "to all those principles, laws and

usages which have obtained currency among civilized states",
almost from the time of the American Revolution; and from
about that time, during the years between the 1760s and the
outbreak of the French Revolution, it came to be regarded in
the same light, as is clear from their writings and speeches, by
British politicians.[1] By this second date the book was entering
upon its long service in this capacity in most of the Foreign
Offices of Europe where it was now generally assumed for
the first time that there was a well-known international law,
the public law of Europe, and that Vattel had collected and
digested it.

It may be objected that there is at least one consideration
which destroys the significance of this last development. How
could Foreign Offices have adopted any earlier compilation
than Vattel's in this way when Foreign Offices themselves had
not been developed and organized much before Vattel's time
—when in England, for example, the existence of the modern
Foreign Office dates only from the 1780s? But this very fact
serves to show how this decisive shift, if this analysis of it is
tolerably correct, was produced by the completion of fundamental changes in the character of Europe's communities and
in the structure of its interstate relations. Up to the eighteenth
century internal social structures and regional divisions had
everywhere remained too strong, and systems of government,
state frontiers and organizational techniques had everywhere
remained insufficiently consolidated, to permit that degree of
governmental development and of central regulation of the
community, and those controlled governmental attitudes to

---

[1] *See* for example an appendix in BURKE'S, *Remarks on the Policy of the Allies
with respect to France* (1793), *Burke's Works*, Bohn edn., Vol. 3, pp. 45–6, and
FOX's speech of January, 1794, printed in *Speeches of Charles James Fox* (1815),
Vol. V, p. 156, in which he criticized the disposition to "throw Vattel and
Grotius into the sea" when their principles disagreed with one's own interests.
For these references I am indebted to Mr. Peter Lyon of the London School
of Economics and Political Science.

intercommunity rivalries, which were required before such a
shift could take place. During the eighteenth century, if only
in Europe, three of the most powerful forces in subsequent
history at last became sufficiently pronounced to bring this
about. The consolidation of the community; the accompanying rise of organized government; the underlying advance of
science and technology—these processes which had been at
work for centuries but which had hitherto moved forward at
only a slow pace, with only limited effects, now underwent
that leap forward or "take-off" which has given a dynamic,
interlocking quality to their subsequent development and
brought about a continuous increase in their impact on
societies. It is true that, as yet, as for a long time to come, their
impact remained uneven as between the different European
societies, for they were accelerating at various times and at
different speeds in different countries. But during the eighteenth century—until the second half of the nineteenth century,
indeed, if we exclude the primacy temporarily achieved by
France under the first Napoleon—even this unequal progress
helped to level up an old, dynastic and highly unequal distribution of relative power within the European states' system,
and to expand that system geographically.

In the two major results of the wars of the first half of the
eighteenth century—the break-up of the traditional Spanish-
Habsburg power complex and the exhaustion of France, the
traditional rival of the Habsburgs and of Spain—and in the
other major developments of that period—this was the time
when Russia emerged as a constant factor in European international politics, when Prussia acquired the rank of a European
power, when Great Britain's rise to the position of a leading
power substituted Anglo-French rivalry for the old Habsburg–
French struggle as the pivot of international relations—Europe
was experiencing not merely the consequences of diplomatic
and other ability and of the play of military fortune, but also

the influence of these more fundamental developments and especially the influence of their uneven rates of advance in its different parts. It was ultimately on this account that during the first half of the eighteenth century the continent was approaching a condition of greater near-equality between a larger number of leading states than it had ever known in its history. And it was for this same reason, it may be suggested, no less than because its leading communities were becoming more integrated and more subject to increasingly centralized and efficient governments, that European international relations exhibited during the second half of the eighteenth century the first unmistakable signs of movement beyond what we have called a primitive condition into what we have termed their post-primitive phase.

It is easy to find other evidence that might make one sceptical of this analysis. How, for example, is the Napoleonic interlude to be explained? Yet just as it is not to be expected that a transformation of this magnitude would establish itself except on the basis of preliminary development over a long period of years, so it is not to be wondered at if its completion was soon followed by a determined effort to undo it. We should not be surprised to find that, while Grotius was pleading for a departure from primitive conduct as early as 1625, Fénelon was still pleading for this a century later and Napoleon, on such a different level of politics, was attempting at the beginning of the nineteenth century, after yet another hundred years, to restore the primitive or imperial pattern from which Europe had so recently escaped and in which France had till recently been so powerful. We may note, indeed, that Napoleon was naturally tempted to return to the imperial goal when the French Revolution, by making her the first country in Europe to accomplish a startling stride towards the integrated community and the modern state, restored France to primacy so soon after the transformation to the post-primitive age had begun. In the same way, to take another possible objection, it is not difficult to understand why, during the resettlement of Europe after Napoleon's downfall, the policies of Western European governments, under the leadership of Great Britain, were based on acceptance of the notions of the sovereign independence and sovereign equality of all states, whereas those of the Russian Tsar, the ruler of the least developed state in Europe, harked back to the federal projects of the sixteenth and seventeenth centuries. These projects were originally propounded before the modern state had approached to its full proportions and before the idea of sovereignty had emerged in all its clarity. Their original object had been the reconstruction by pacific means of the single empire of Europe that had been the logical, the inexorable aim when the international system was composed of segmentary communities governed by primitive states. If they were now misunderstood as having been plans for peace, and as still being the only means of achieving peace among post-primitive states, this was because the influence of new conditions and of new ideas was necessarily slow to affect the outlook of the less developed and more peripheral of the states.

Far more impressive, indeed, that these reminders of an earlier age is the fact that, after the downfall of Napoleon in 1815 and with the victory within a few more years of Castlereagh's ideas over Alexander I's conception of the Holy Alliance and of the Congress system, these older notions were never again to be embraced by governments. From the early years of the nineteenth century the concept of sovereignty, with the implications which that involved when it was applied to the international situation, became the central principle in the external policy and the international conduct of all the leading states in the European system. So much was this so that, as is customary when men have finally adopted a

fundamental idea, the solution of all problems and the adjustment to all new developments were made to conform to it.
In Europe itself these more advanced governments insisted
that every political structure must be a state like themselves—
so that they could not settle the international status of the
Holy See without resorting to the device of establishing a
Vatican city state—and that each state must be sovereign in its
independence and in terms of its equality with other states.
And when these principles were inapplicable to circumstances
in Europe, or incapable of solving problems there, they insisted that the only alternative was the opposite of sovereignty,
its conscious negation indeed—the neutralization of minor
states and of disputed or buffer regions. In areas beyond
Europe, into which they were now extending their activities
more rapidly than before, they similarly thought and acted
within the categories of statehood and sovereignty as far as
the very different conditions which prevailed there would
permit.

Up to the seventeenth century, Europeans had expanded
into these areas either on the principle that, because they were
inhabited by pagans, Africa, Asia and America were empty
lands, open for acquisition by the Christian, dynastic, legitim-
ist governments of Europe, or else—where total acquisition
had been impracticable, as in the Ottoman Empire or in the
Indian Empire of the Great Mogul—through the development
of special arrangments which enabled them to operate in the
very different social and political circumstances which they
found there. Thus, while Christian opinion had been shocked
by the diplomatic relations which France developed with the
Turk after the beginning of the seventeenth century, European
governments and traders had not hesitated to accept the
capitulations system which permitted those Europeans who
lived in the Sultan's lands to be fitted into the ordinary structure of government for the non-Muslim subjects of his

Empire. The Companies through which they did their work in India had easily accepted, in the same way, a kind of vassal relationship with the Great Mogul. But after the 1820s—after the aspiration of the Holy Alliance to restore the European dynastic system against the revolt of Spain's colonies in Latin America had called forth the Monroe doctrine and foundered on the opposition of Great Britain—the European outlook upon the extra-European areas rapidly became one which instinctively applied the concept of the sovereign state and the notion of international sovereignty to conditions in which these ideas remained alien ideas.

We cannot but be struck by the rigidity of this approach when we see the British Resident advising the native chiefs of New Zealand in the 1830s to form themselves into a state to be called "The United Tribes of New Zealand"[1]; or read in the report of one Captain Jones on one of the Yoruba tribal states of West Africa in 1861 that it was necessary to give an account of "the Constitution" of "this Power" before proceeding to describe its military forces;[2] or study the difficulties which followed when the Western governments, on the assumption that wherever there were recognizable political authorities they must be modern rulers in modern states, confused the powers of the Japanese Tycoon with those of the Mikado, or insisted that the solution to the Eastern Question after the Crimean war lay in imposing on the Sultan of Turkey the rights and duties of admission to the circle of the European Great Powers, or made treaty arrangements with North American Indian tribes, with potentates in Persia, India, Malaya, Siam and Borneo, and with African tribal leaders. If we are tempted to dismiss this outlook as naïve, however,

---

[1] See CLIVE PARRY, *Nationality and Citizenship Laws of the Commonwealth* (1957), Vol. 1, p. 608. I am indebted to Dr. Clive Parry for pointing out this example.

[2] J. F. ADE AJAYI and ROBERT S. SMITH, *Yoruba Warfare in the Nineteenth Century* (1964), p. 132.

we must remember that it is still as firmly applied today as ever it was, and far more widely, in circumstances to which, in many parts of the world, it is no more applicable than it was a century and more ago.

It must be added, moreover, that on the basis of government acceptance of the principles of state sovereignty and independence, themselves the outcome of its own decisive transformation during the years between the Seven Years' War and the Congress of Vienna, the European international system was made to register further advances and at least some genuine extension during the remainder of the nineteenth century as a result of government recognition that these principles involved limits on freedom of action. This is not the place to consider these achievements in detail.[1] It is sufficient to note that, if the foundations of the modern system of international law were laid as late as during the second half of the eighteenth century, governments did not take long thereafter to accomplish the first modern international political settlement at the Congress of Vienna. It was a settlement which, as well as giving first expression to the principle of free navigation on international rivers and laying down the rules which still regulate the ranks of diplomatic envoys, determined the frontiers of nearly every state in Europe, gave every signatory the right to uphold its terms and was regarded as a single instrument, no part of which could be infringed without invalidating the rest. In the generation after 1815, first in the Congress system and then in the shape of the Concert of the European Powers, they gave its first form to that political machinery of which an international system stands in need in modern conditions. With the Concert idea to aid them they produced the first great expansion of modern international law, jurisdiction and administration, which occurred during

[1] For a detailed treatment *see* F. H. HINSLEY, *Power and the Pursuit of Peace* (1963), Part II.

the second half of the nineteenth century, and established the principle that newly recognized states beyond Europe and the United States of America—states like Japan—should be bound by the whole existing body of international law, including the rules developed before these states came into existence and the usages developed in the different civilization of Europe.

The Abuse of the Concept and the Attempt to Dispense with it in Conditions of International Disorder

In the early years of the twentieth century the more advanced governments went still further. After the First World War, in the experiment with the League of Nations, they embarked upon the ambitious—and then at least, we may add, impossible—task of restricting their own sovereign independence by legal limits and institutional means. The experiment was undertaken as a result of the moral shock and the material destruction administered by the outbreak and the conduct of the First World War, as the Congress system and the Concert of Europe had been launched on the momentum of men's reaction against their experiences during the war with Napoleon. But it owed its character to more fundamental developments.

Already from the time of Hegel—from the time when the concept was at last being received in the practice of states and made into the basis of a working international system—there had slowly re-emerged in the realm of political theory a disposition to force the international implications of the sovereignty of the state to absolute extremes. From about 1870 the influence of Hegel's ideas—of his conception of the state as the realization of the moral idea and as an absolute end; of his insistence that, since there is no other law for the state but the purpose of its own self, the relation between states must be a relation of "independencies" which may stipulate among themselves but which remain above all stipulations; of his thesis that, as sovereignty is the true essence of the state, it is especially in the right to make war that this sovereignty manifests itself—had markedly increased. Nor was it only in Germany, where they were propagated with especial ruthlessness by writers like Treitschke, Lasson, Kaufmann and Jellinek, that these ideas gained ground. In all states it now became an established if not an unquestioned doctrine that, since moral relations presuppose an organized life and since such a life exists only under the state, therefore, to quote the English idealist philosopher Bosanquet, "there can be no violation of law by the state";[1] and in international law the universal trend was one of approximation to the Hegelian conception of the state and of its sovereignty. And then, secondly, and not unconnected with this movement in thought, there had begun to take place from about the same time a change in the quality of the relations between the Great Powers. A deterioration in their conduct and an intensification of their rivalries now emphasized that, despite all its achievements since the beginning of the nineteenth century, the international system remained incapable of averting the increasingly alarming danger of a reversion to war.

Since the 1880s accelerating rates of advance towards the integrated community, in the organization of government and in scientific and technological ability, and the increasingly disproportionate advance of these processes within the different societies, had been producing, both as between the more developed states themselves and as between them and the undeveloped parts of the world, distortions in a distribution of relative power which had been basically stable since 1815. This development had expressed itself first in the great burst of modern oversea imperialism which occurred from that time and then in the grave unsettlement which characterized

[1] BERNARD BOSANQUET, *Philosophical Theory of the State* (4th edn., 1923), pp. 302–4.

the relations between even the Great Powers from the beginning of the twentieth century. It is not for nothing, we may add at this point, that the federal German Empire, the most disturbing single element among the many which underlay these deteriorations, was the least integrated as a community and the worst organized as to its government system, but also the most dynamic as a scientific and technological structure, of all the leading states of the time. It was for these two reasons that when the international system broke down, and when with the onset and in the aftermath of the World War the international problem began to be termed the international anarchy, the conviction that it was necessary to limit or even abolish the sovereign independence of the separate state by institutional means, and in the last resort by military sanctions, was more widely accepted as containing the ultimate wisdom than it had been in any previous age.

This movement of opinion—it would perhaps be too much to say that it was a movement in thought—played a decisive part in shaping the League of Nations. It was also instrumental in ensuring the failure of the experiment. At one level this failure is explained by the fact that, while some governments went some way towards adopting its federal or confederal premises, the resulting organization was unable even to narrow the gap between these premises and the practice of states that in most men's minds it was designed to close. Not only did other governments make only a pretence or not even a pretence of accepting them. Not only was there added to this the unfavourable circumstance that the condition of international unsettlement which had produced the World War had in any case been intensified by the War's results. Even those governments which were favourably disposed were unable fully to adopt these premises on account of the nature of the modern community and the responsibilities of the modern state. At a more fundamental level of explanation, indeed, the League of Nations failed in its task for this other reason. It sought to solve the international problem, to avoid in particular the recurrence of war, by the suppression or the limitation by external means of the sovereignty of the individual state at a time when the outstanding development of recent history had been the increase in the power, the scope and the efficiency of the individual state—not to speak of its indispensability in the modern community.

In logic, perhaps, there was nothing preposterous about such an enterprise, especially when it was assumed that the increase in the power and efficiency of the state was the root cause of the increase in international unsettlement and in the destructiveness of war during the past hundred years. But this assumption confused causation with coincidence: the increase in destructiveness and unsettlement had been a product of the same underlying developments as those which had enlarged the scope of the state. And even if this assumption had been correct, the enterprise would still have foundered because its underlying thesis was also derived from two more ancient and outmoded streams of thought.

Of these sources of inspiration the older had originated when men had still sought the reconstruction of the single empire or federation of Europe. Schemes to this end—an understandable aim, perhaps, in the days when Europe's states had been primitive states—were now misapplied to the task of achieving peace between post-primitive communities. The other was the assumption, first developed during the eighteenth-century Enlightenment, that at least some of the communities of the world were already developed beyond the post-primitive stage—the conviction which led President Wilson, like Bentham and other *Philosophes* of that earlier date, to believe that at least a League based on the civilized or democratic nations must succeed. But this assumption, though less hoary than the antique federal goal, was despite this fact still premature; and in addition those who held to it were torn between the desire to establish and a disposition to distrust a federal organization that would itself become sovereign, if successful. The resulting League ideology was a superficial synthesis which omitted all serious analysis either of the function of the doctrine of sovereignty or of the achievements of the international system in the period since the formulation of that doctrine had announced that that system had entered its modern phase.

The message involved in the emergence of that doctrine—it was implicit already in the thought of Bodin and Grotius, explicit by the time of Fénelon and Vattel—was that the separate community and its sovereign state, which had the deepest roots in the past, would also have the deepest relevance long into the future, and that the elimination of international disorder would only come, if it ever came, through an increase in the caution, the wisdom and the responsibility of the separate communities and states. The lessons to be derived from the subsequent development of the international system are equally plain. If we look for the explanation of the advances made by that system since the middle of the eighteenth century we shall find that it lies in the fact that progress was made whenever governments recognized the need for individual responsibility as the basis for common collaboration in a multilateral system of states—even if it is also a fact that on each occasion this recognition was being forced upon governments by their renewed experience of the risks of uncontrolled behaviour and by their growing awareness of the complexity of their own needs. We shall acquire, indeed, a renewed respect for the percipience of Immanuel Kant who, in the 1780s and 1790s, spelling out clearly the message that peace could now be founded only on self-imposed improvement in the conduct of the independent sovereign state, was the first to add to it, on the basis of some insight into the history and nature of the community and the state, both a warning and a ground for optimism.

His warning was that the world would have to wait for this improvement until its communities and their governments had passed beyond what he would have called their pre-constitutional days—what we have termed their post-primitive stage. His ground for optimism—discerned in the early days of the post-primitive stage in Europe but with some awareness that Europe had already, if not long since, embarked upon it—was contained in his insistence that by the movement of the communities towards diversification and greater inter-dependence of needs, of international relations towards greater complexity, and of warfare towards higher and higher levels of destructiveness, the states would be forced in time to evolve beyond that stage, and thus to advance in their international conduct.

VI

THE CONCEPT OF SOVEREIGNTY IN
THE MODERN WORLD

WHEN we contemplate the most recent phase in the history
of politics and of political theory we cannot but be struck by
a divergence which has grown up perhaps since Rousseau's
time, certainly during the past hundred years, where the
sovereignty concept is concerned.

In the realm of politics, at least in the developing areas of the
world, these years have witnessed a greater and more continuous increase in the integration of the political community
and the power of the state than was achieved in all previous
history. By whatever means they were advanced—whether by
gradual changes in the basis of government as in England
from the 1830s, or by a succession of changes in the form of
government as in France from the 1840s, or by more violent
revolution in the aftermath of international war as in Russia
since 1917—the outstanding processes in these areas have been
the centralization of the community and the associated rise of
the centralizing state. At whatever date they began to register
themselves in the various communities, and regardless of the
varying rapidity of their development, the basic forces producing them have in each case been those technical and
economic changes which have steadily transformed the
quality of political and social existence since the beginning of
the nineteenth century, and which continue to transform it
in the same directions.

The final establishment of sovereignty as the dominant
concept in the field of working political assumptions has been

a natural reflection of these processes. For wherever they have occurred they have resulted in a closer association between the community and the state. It may be said indeed that they have resulted in this inevitably—so inevitably that it has been accomplished by revolution, by the physical overthrow of established régimes, whenever the necessary adjustment of government forms and attitudes has been found to be impossible by gradual or reformist methods—and that the dominance of the sovereignty assumption has been no less inevitably another of their results. Nor is there any sign that this dominance, dating back to the early nineteenth century, is yet weakening. In international law as in international practice the quality of sovereignty in the separate community is not only still generally held to be the essential qualification for full membership of the international community; it is still necessarily held to be so. The internal mechanism of the separate modern community would similarly grind to a halt if the assumption were abandoned or widely disbelieved—and so much so that in the modern community its abandonment remains impossible.

The divergence which has been referred to is not a divergence, then, between political practice and this working assumption on which political practice is based. It is a divergence between that practice and its most prominent underlying assumption on the one hand and political theorizing on the other. For in the field of political theory there has developed during this same period a prominent tendency to disapprove of sovereignty as an immoral concept, or to dismiss it as an outmoded concept, or at least to regard it as a thesis requiring fundamental revision on one or the other or on both of these grounds.

In any attempt to explain this divergence and to assess this critical tendency considerable weight must be given to the prevalence of the element of moral disapproval. When Laski contended in 1941 that "it would be of lasting benefit to political science if the whole concept of sovereignty were surrendered" he supported this contention with, among other arguments, the statement that "it is at least probable that it has dangerous moral consequences".[1] He was here repeating what a succession of political theorists have concluded about internal sovereignty with ever-increasing conviction, and less caution, since the middle of the nineteenth century, and he was expressing sentiments which many theorists still uphold. In connexion with sovereignty in its international aspect the growth of disapproval has been even more pronounced, especially during the past fifty years. Kant's warning that men's hopes for international peace must be based on the prospect of increased self-discipline on the part of independent communities and states, and that these hopes might be long deferred, was never much pondered after Kant had issued it. From the early years of the twentieth century it was quite lost to sight—Kant's entire argument was misunderstood, indeed —when increasing numbers of increasingly desperate men, in admittedly deteriorating international conditions, made the independent state their scapegoat, the doctrine of sovereignty their bugbear and varying approaches to international government their overriding and their impracticable objective.

More than one reason for the growth of this element of moral disapproval suggest themselves. But perhaps the most powerful will be found to be the preoccupation of many of the critics of the sovereignty thesis with things as they ought to be, or as they would like them to be, rather than with things as things are. They have usually been not political scientists, or not political scientists merely, so much as political theorists interested in changing political conditions or at least in reforming prevailing assumptions about these conditions. This interest is not to be deplored for itself: the most profound of

[1] HAROLD J. LASKI, *The Grammar of Politics* (1941), pp. 44–5.

political thinkers have shared it. But so have those who must be ranked among the most superficial. What counts in this matter, what gives relevance and ensures success to the effort to revise the conditions and the presuppositions of political activity, is the extent to which political theory remains in touch with political science—with the facts. Like the successful practical statesman, the perceptive critical theorist works with the grain. And the truth is that many of the critics of sovereignty have been more distinguished for their fervour for change than for their understanding of the underlying conditions and trends in actual politics. In order to see this truth we have only to consider the fate of the Marxist conviction that the state would wither away once society was fully reorganized on socialist premises; or the futility of all those schemes which, from Rousseau's desire to reconstitute the city state to Laski's advocacy of pluralism, have sought a solution to the problems of political organization in the decentralization of the modern territorial community; or, to take another example, the equally well established impracticability of all the proposals for terminating the international anarchy by the establishment of international government, or at least of some strong international organization, which have gained such wide support since men like Lowes Dickinson revived them during the First World War. In each of these directions the knowledge that problems existed was not accompanied by any marked understanding of their source, their nature and their complexity. The abandonment of sovereignty, advance beyond sovereignty, was proposed as the cure; but the cure was proceeded by no adequate diagnosis of the disease.

At the same time, it must be conceded that the critics were right to conclude that the problems they were hoping to solve did and do exist. It may be added that they have not been wholly wrong in discerning a connexion between these problems and the victory of the concept of sovereignty in the

P

field of working political assumptions. For during the period which has witnessed this victory and the associated rise of the modern state the advocates of the state have been no less inclined than the critics to indulge in theorizing which has borne little relation to the significance which must be given to the concept of sovereignty if that concept is properly understood.

When Marx argued that it was the proper and predestined course of political development that the political society should annihilate the state he was reacting against Hegel's equally Messianic contention that its proper and predestined course was one by which a nation was absorbed by, was turned into, a state. Ever since Hegel's time the tendency of some political theorists to moralize against the state and the concept of sovereignty has been matched by an equally steady tendency among other theorists to moralize in defence of them—to treat the state or nation as an absolute end and the principle of sovereignty as the principle which either gives to the state or the nation absolute power or symbolizes their actual possession of such power. Nor can there be any doubt that this tendency to exalt the power of the state and the quality of sovereignty was instrumental in intensifying the opposite disposition to regard the concept of sovereignty as being morally dangerous. In the past hundred years, both within and between communities, men have often indulged in the excessive or the dubious use of political power. This use or misuse of power would have occurred if the concept of sovereignty had never been formulated, as it did before the concept was formulated. But because it was now condoned or justified in some quarters by reference to that concept, the concept itself was in other quarters understandably brought into disrepute.

But if this was an understandable reaction it was neither a necessary nor a logical one. What was required of the critics of sovereignty was not the conclusion to which they have been so powerfully drawn—the conclusion that a concept which was being put to morally dubious uses was for that reason a morally dangerous concept—but the realization that this exaltation of the concept involved a distortion of its real significance and true function. If their own moralism, their preoccupation with things as they would have liked them to be, was one reason for the growing disapproval of the concept of sovereignty, another and no less important one was their lack of sufficient understanding of the nature and function of this concept whose influence they blamed for the ills of the world.

The concept of sovereignty, as we have already stressed, is not in terms of its history or in terms of political science a concept which may properly be used to explain—let alone to justify—whatever the state or the political society does or may choose to do. It is a principle which maintains no more than that there must be a supreme authority within the political community if the community is to exist at all, or at least if it is to be able to act as its character and circumstances require it to do. It may well be only too easy to slip from this proper interpretation into that improper or absolutist use of it which has been so prevalent in recent times. The evidence of history certainly establishes that the modern democratic or constitutional state has been no less prone to make this distortion than were the personal rulerships which sought to harness the concept to the chariot of an absolute emperor in the days of Rome or to the wagon of Divine Right in the concept's early modern days. Yet it remains the case that to make this transition is to misunderstand the function of sovereignty; and it is equally the case that a misunderstanding of the concept on the part of those who have questioned its validity, their acceptance of the misuse of it by those who have distorted its true meaning in the interests of power, has been a second powerful factor behind the increase of moral disapproval.

It has been no less instrumental in producing that other

modern attitude which has dismissed sovereignty as an out-
dated thesis. This conviction has often proceeded, it is true,
from moralism *tout court*: the conclusion that an assumption
which is judged to be morally dangerous is for that reason also
outworn is prevalent in circles which are preoccupied with
things as things ought to be. With more serious critics of
sovereignty, however, these two grounds of criticism have
normally been separated. Laski, for example, maintained not
only that sovereignty probably had dangerous moral consequences but also, and as a distinct argument, that it was "of
dubious correctness in fact",[1] and since Laski's day the increasing involvement of political thought in facts rather than in
opinion, in analysis rather than in speculation, in science rather
than in theory, has yielded a host of commentaries in which
the theory of sovereignty is found to fit far from perfectly, if
at all, with the character, the mechanism and the operation of
the modern political community. The chief grounds on which
even these professional circles have based this finding are
twofold. One is the argument, to which we shall turn later,
that the internal structure of the modern community has
become so complex, its mode of operation so diverse and
ramified, its distribution of power so dispersed, that it is
impossible either to suppose that there is a single sovereign
authority within it or to suppose that this assumption is any
longer made. The other is the erroneous argument that since
the community or the state is no longer wholly self-sufficient
if it ever was—since it is in various directions inhibited and
denied utter freedom of action as a result of the increased
complexity of the wider international context—it can no
longer be accredited with the possession of sovereign power.
And the fallacy underlying this second argument is that same
misinterpretation of the concept of sovereignty to which we
have just drawn attention.

[1] op. cit., pp. 44–5.

The argument is not wrong in its belief that the physical, moral and legal limits on the freedom of the individual community and state have markedly closed in recent times as a result of changes in the interstate or intercommunity environment. Paradoxically, perhaps, the power and also the impotence of the community and the state have mounted simultaneously in a single process: these changes in international conditions have proceeded from precisely those technical, social and economic forces which have been producing the highly integrated community and the modern state. This fact is vividly illustrated by the almost poignant situation in which, at exactly that stage when the efficiency and the functions of the community and the state had expanded to the highest point in all their history, these organizations have recently become powerless in the central function of protecting their inhabitants against the use by other communities and states of the latest weapons. It may be taken for granted that this and other physical inroads into their freedom and competence will soon be reflected in legal and moral changes in the context and character of international conduct. It appears to be the case that international law has already made the adjustment by ceasing to regard the right of war as a legal right—by casting out war from the body of legal concepts. It is not impossible that the destruction of the capacity to defend the community is now combining with such other developments as highly intensified technological, financial and economic interdependence to render further military conflict between advanced communities not only extra-legal but also as morally unthinkable as it is physically hazardous. But it is wrong to conclude from these changes in the international environment and from these predictable effects on the texture of international conduct that the concept of sovereignty has now ceased to be either an accurate reflection of the international condition or a valid central assumption in international relations. To argue in this way is to equate the attribute of sovereignty with the possession of unfettered freedom of action and the validity of the concept of sovereignty with the absence of restraints on power. To do that is to confuse the situation to which the claimants of sovereignty may often have aspired, indeed, with the opposite condition, with the absence of isolation and total freedom, in which the concept, especially in its international version, could alone acquire and can alone retain its relevance.

It is not only in logic that this argument is inaccurate, but also in fact. In the past half century, in response to the growing complexities of international conditions and as a result of the increasing sophistication of international lawyers, governments have become less wedded than during the nineteenth century to the view that sovereignty is the sole concept that can be applied to international problems. In the development of ideas underlying the Mandates system after the First World War, in their extension of these in the Trusteeship system after the Second World War, and still more recently in the Antarctic Treaty of 1959 (embodying the agreement that "no new claim, or enlargement of an existing claim, to territorial sovereignty . . . shall be asserted while the present Treaty is in force"[1]) and their approach to the problem of South West Africa, they have shown a disposition to agree that there may be other solutions to international problems than the acquisition and asertion of sovereignty or the imposition of neutral status. We cannot overlook the extent to which Mandate and Trusteeship ideas were an unavoidable compromise or the fact that South West Africa and Antarctica happen to be areas of small international significance; but this more flexible attitude remains a factor to be reckoned with. If men could discover another new continent it is not impossible that they would handle the resulting complications in such a way as to

[1] Cmnd. 1953, Treaty Series No. 97 (1961), Article IV.

avoid the over-simple certitudes which accompanied the nineteenth-century scramble for Africa; and it is not impossible that this hypothetical speculation will be borne out by the way in which they will handle the complications arising from the exploration of outer space. But it is one thing to recognize that sovereignty is ceasing to be the sole international concept and quite another thing to argue that it is ceasing to be the central concept.

To the cautionary words already issued on this score we must add this further warning. The more flexible attitude of recent years was foreshadowed during the last quarter of the nineteenth century, when attachment to the doctrine of sovereignty was at its height, by the enforced adoption of such devices as the early international régimes set up to administer the Egyptian debt in 1876, the Suez Canal in 1883 and the Congo Free State in 1885; the protectorate that was so extensively used in Africa; the condominium that was applied to the Sudan and the New Hebrides; the protected semi-sovereign state that was resorted to in North Africa, in Malaya and on the North West Frontier of India; and, not least important, the multifarious techniques which transformed parts of the British Empire into the British Commonwealth of self-governing Dominions. For this reason if for no others it would be incautious to deny that, as we have said already, the sovereignty of the individual community and state continues to be necessarily the essential qualification for membership of the international community in practice no less than in law. And by way of substantiating this statement it is sufficient to draw attention to two sources of the confusion which characterizes modern international thinking—a confusion which would be much reduced if they were better understood.

This statement is so much a statement of fact that, with the continued geographical expansion of the international system, it still proves impossible to avoid the nineteenth-century practice of insisting that the quality of sovereignty be granted for international purposes to newly independent areas in which sovereignty has not yet become the relevant or even a possible expression of internal political development and conditions. It is so much a statement of fact that, to turn from these undeveloped areas to another source of international misunderstanding, to the efforts of the advanced communities of the world to make progress with the establishment of an international political organization, it contains all that is required to explain the stultification of these efforts.

In a summary of the historical evolution of municipal law from its primitive beginnings Kelsen once pointed out that in the applying of law the judicial procedure—the process of reaching a decision on the facts of the case—has always been centralized before the executive procedure—the execution of the sanction against the culprit—in which the principle of self-help long resisted the power of a central state administration; and, further, that the centralization in the hands of the state of the functions involved in applying law has always preceded the centralization of the function of creating it. Within the separate territorial community, courts were established to apply customary law, which derived its forms from the collaboration of the inhabitants, long before the emergence of legislative organs with the power to make additional law. "A legal community which has courts and an administration is a state, but a central organ of legislation is not a requisite of a state. . . . As soon as the position of chief becomes a permanent institution . . . the chief appears as judge, not as legislator."[1] He argued that this order of evolution, so ubiquitous as to suggest that it reflects the sociological and the socio-psychological nature of law, must probably be followed in the historical development of international law.

[1] KELSEN, *Law and Peace* (1942), pp. 145–8.

And no student of the facts of that development as it has so far proceeded will disagree with the conclusions he advanced on the basis of this hypothesis: that "these facts show clearly that the law of the interstate community develops in the same direction as the primitive law of the pre-state community"; that "they also suggest . . . that the first step towards an enduring peace must be the establishment of an international community the members of which are obliged to submit all disputes . . . to a permanent international court and to respect the decisions of this authority"; that "until this end has been attained . . . the other much more far-reaching one cannot possibly be achieved, namely, the establishment of a community of states subjected to a central administration with centralized executive power at its disposal, or even the establishment of a federal world state with a world-wide administration and a world legislature."[1]

When the historian contemplates, indeed, the efforts made in the twentieth century to proceed directly from the present-day international system, which remains politically de-centralized, to forms of centrally organized executive and legislative power like a strong United Nations, a United Europe or the Common Market, he is disposed to add another conclusion: that the similarity between municipal and inter-national evolution breaks down only if it is assumed that the international condition, sharing these characteristics with the primitive municipal condition, must necessarily ever proceed to the same sophisticated culmination in the achievement of the fully executive and legislative state. It seems more likely that Kant was right—that the international system is a political system *sui generis*—in which case things will find an adequate culmination if ever an international court arrives to complete the international rule of law. But to enter upon this debate would be an academic exercise. It is sufficient for the present

[1] ibid., pp. 148–50.

argument to be clear on points which are less open to dispute.

The attainment of even Kant's less visionary goal of a rule of law between sovereign states still lies far in the future. And the reason for this is not to be found simply in the fact that most efforts to improve the international system in the past fifty years have taken a more ambitious and an even less immediately practicable course. It lies in the fact that the separate territorial and cultural community remains the most appropriate frame—the sole viable frame, indeed—for the conduct of political life and for the conservation and expression of political as of economic and technical power. It lies in the fact that the forms of the separate centralized state remain the most appropriate, indeed the only viable, means of organizing this conduct and this power, as also of controlling and disciplining them. Nor is it merely the case that these facts remain true. Recent and continuing changes in technology and in economic and social conditions have subjected the international freedom and independence of the community and the state to considerable erosion. It is more than possible that these changes will one day compel at least the more advanced communities and states to establish and respect the international court which is the logical method of rationalizing their relations in that stage to which they have now evolved. But it must also be remembered that simultaneously these changes have greatly increased the cohesion of the community and greatly expanded the functions and the power of the state.

This erosion has no bearing, as we have seen, on the international validity of the concept of sovereignty. If it is indeed the case that war is ceasing to be a legal right, this validity will remain unimpaired; and not even the rationalization of the changing context of international relations that would result from the establishment of an effective court would be incompatible with or destructive of it. A sovereign power may choose to subscribe to limitations without ceasing to be sovereign. On the other hand, this increased integration of the community and this expanded role and power of the state, which have ensured the dominance of the concept during recent times, and which will preserve its international relevance for a long time to come, continue also to ensure its validity within the modern separate community. It is from its recognition of this truth that the recent thinking of the Secretary-General of the United Nations' Organization, to the effect that the Organization must acquire the resources and the attributes of a state if it is to succeed in carrying out the peace-keeping function it was established to perform, derives its ironical and self-destructive logic.[1] We must accordingly consider why not only the international but also the internal relevance and accuracy of the sovereignty thesis has been so much questioned.

The central argument here we have already stated: the internal structure of the modern community has become so ramified, its modes of operation so varied, its distribution of power and influence so dispersed, that it is incorrect either to suppose that there is a single sovereign authority within it or to suppose that the existence of such an authority is any longer assumed. We may now add that a marked increase in the internal complexity of the community and the state has without doubt come about within the last hundred years, both in parallel with the increased integration of the community and the expanded functions of the state and as a result of the closer association between the community and the state which has expressed itself in the rise of mass politics and popular forms of government. The argument is mistaken, however, in assuming that this complexity has increased to such an extent that it has destroyed the particular community-state relationship which found its necessary expression in the formulation

[1] *The Times*, London, 7th August, 1965.

of the sovereignty thesis. All the evidence goes to show that
this particular relationship, which will give relevance to that
thesis so long as it persists, has remained undisturbed.

When Laski argued that the concept of sovereignty was "of
dubious correctness in fact" he meant, as he went on to say,
that there was evidence that the sovereign state, one way of
organizing the use of power in the community, was a way of
doing this "whose utility has now reached its apogee". But it
was not on the basis of facts that he arrived at this judgement
so much as from the conviction that "there is historically no
limit to the variety of ways in which the use of power may be
organized".[1] And this conviction is fallacious. Historically, at
any rate, the number of ways of organizing political power
has been severely restricted. All evolution from primitive
pre-state methods has been inexorably towards the establishment and the consolidation of the state whenever this evolution has occurred; and this is so much the case that two
propositions may be confidently laid down in relation to the
more advanced political communities in which the forms of
the state, having made their appearance long ago, have also
achieved that degree of consolidation which has been characteristic of them in recent times. Before these state forms can
be so seriously weakened as to be superseded by others, before
this community-state relationship can be destroyed, these
communities must either be subjected to the strain of so much
complexity that they retreat to the segmentary condition
which prevailed before the consolidation of the state, or they
must make so much further internal advance that we cannot
yet attempt to portray the post-state form of organization that
will be the appropriate successor to the state. And before either
of these processes can even begin to take place these communities must experience, over a prolonged period of time,
far greater changes in conditions than those which have so far

[1] LASKI, op. cit., pp. 44-5.

been imposed on them. For if we now turn to the evidence we have no difficulty in seeing that the community-state relationship that has long been established in modern societies, far from being undermined, has been consolidated by its increasing complexity.

On the one hand, it is this increasing complexity, springing equally from the growing integration of the community and the growing role and power of the state, which has preserved the more advanced communities from reversion to segmentary politics by necessitating the popularization of government and by emphasizing in other ways also the mutual dependence of community and state. Empires have sundered under the impact of this process. Historical political structures of a more compact and cohesive character than empires have been deprived of territories—as was, to take but one example, the United Kingdom of a part of Ireland. But within borders which have continued to circumscribe single political communities the process has worked in the opposite direction whenever the community has been one which had surmounted the hump which constitutes the division between the segmentary and the unitary stage. Not only is normal political dissension easily contained within the mould of the state. In recent times not even the resort to extra-legal action in revolutionary conditions, while it has sometimes changed the form of government, has ever in advancing unitary communities either aimed at or succeeded in overthrowing the unitary state. Some of these communities are now attempting to offset their perhaps excessive centralization by the devolution of administration and authority to regional bodies; but all such schemes emanate from the central authority and remain integral parts of a central plan. Even of federal communities what was not true of earlier times has become true in the past hundred years: the federal form of state is always a unitary form of state in the process of formation or dissolution. A community subjected to this consolidating process must either move towards this greater integration and this closer association with its state or it must disintegrate into more than one consolidated community.

It is equally clear, on the other hand, that the consolidation of the community-state relationship has nowhere yet come near to destroying either that dichotomy between the community and the forms of the state which we have singled out as one of the essential features of the modern community or that acceptance of the ultimate primacy of the power of the state which we have singled out as the other. The total identification of the community and the state has been the objective of some political theorists since at least the time of Hegel and Marx. From an even earlier date there have been those who, like Rousseau, hoped to achieve this by abolishing the state. But the objective remains unattainable by any route. Confrontation between the community and the forms of its separate state; the state's possession of ultimate power in the community—these remain the strictly necessary conditions of political organization even though it has become a further requirement of political stability that community and state should be intimately associated in multifarious ways.

Historically these conditions have also been the sufficient conditions for the validity, not to say the necessity, of the concept of sovereignty. If it is to be proved that this concept has become either invalid or unnecessary in complex modern communities it must be shown that these conditions no longer exist there—or else that, while continuing to be the basic features of political society, they no longer can be or no longer need to be sustained and justified by the device of assuming that the state wields supreme or sovereign power. But it will be found that all attempts to show that the sovereignty thesis has become outmoded or superfluous, like all attempts to demonstrate the first of these propositions, break down if care is taken to distinguish the fact that the community-state relationship has acquired great complexity and intimacy from the erroneous supposition that these features of the relationship have been obliterated.

It is undoubtedly true that the concept of the state, like its character or its actual forms, has undergone a profound change in consequence of its more intimate relationship with a more complex community. What was once equated with the monarch, or with some other physical body of men who exercised the rulership, has acquired an impersonal, a legal, even a fictional, connotation since the movement towards this closer intimacy and this greater complexity, as illustrated by such developments as the rise of legislatures, the expansion of electorates, the emergence of modern civil services and the dispersal of actual power from the ruler to these and other elements, began to demand that all the elements involved in the business of operating the community should come to be regarded as being merely so many organs of the state itself. This process has been less prominent in the constitutional theory of communities where the problems created by the impossibility of concentrating all the power in either the community or the state have been soluble by political compromise, on the basis of a slow evolution of political forms, than in those in which conflict between the community and the state has resulted in constitutions based on revolution or on frequent changes in the form of government. Not for nothing does sovereignty in England remain with the Crown-in-Parliament, without the need for that still more shadowy and more notional state which is assumed to wield it in some communities. But no advancing community has escaped the process: the English conception of the Crown-in-Parliament has long been far more metaphysical, far less personal, than when it was first fashioned in the sixteenth century.

The operation of the state, the manipulation of the

state-community relationship, has similarly become more complex under the pressure of the same developments. This may be true only of detail and technique. It would be wrong to assume that it has ever been possible to conduct this operation successfully without compromise, tact and delicacy; and it is not impossible that compromise, tact and delicacy have become less important in proportion as the state has become less personal and the community a less recalcitrant thing. Let us admit, however, that the ethical, political and practicability limits which have always inhibited the free use of the state's power have at least acquired greater rigidity and precision from the increased complexity of the community, of the state itself and of the association between the two. Once again, this has been more markedly the case in societies where these processes have been the source of serious conflict between the two. In such societies this fact has secured the establishment of fundamental laws or of written constitutions which expressly limit what the state may do. In England, on the other hand, it remains an academic question, if an important one, whether a decision of the Crown-in-Parliament can bind the future activities of this sovereign authority in terms of their scope or their form. In all societies, even so, these processes have at least resulted in some rules specifying the way in which the state must do what it does. Nor is there any modern state which does not frequently find or judge it to be for political reasons unwise or impossible to act or decide as it would or should. The outstanding characteristic of modern political organization is that problems are perforce permitted to solve themselves—unless it is that they are not solved—even if it is another characteristic of advanced societies that indecisiveness is not disastrous.

It has thus become increasingly possible over the past half century for commentators to dismiss the theory of the sovereignty of the state as a fiction and, looking behind it to what they judge to be the realities of political organization, to pronounce the theory misleading as well as artificial. That since political power is actually widely dispersed, and since the indivisibility and inalienability of ultimate power is one of the marks of sovereignty, the theory of sovereignty has become an inaccurate and an irrelevant theory—a fiction like the state itself. That since, in so far as there remains any ultimate power in the community, it is either difficult to perceive where it actually lies or easy to show that it is actually and often legally severely restricted, again the theory of sovereignty has become inaccurate and irrelevant—the other marks of sovereignty being that it is manifest who possesses this power to command and that he or it is without a superior. That in so far as fictions, even the fiction of sovereignty, perform a necessary function, the theory of sovereignty retains its value only as a legislative and a legal concept, and that it is accordingly imperative to be clear that we move from the sphere of the sovereignty doctrine to the field of mere power politics when we contemplate those operations of the political society which are not concerned with the making and the applying of the law. These, in brief summary, are the main arguments which, coming down to us through volumes of discussion in the past fifty years, have recently become all the more irresistible on account of the spread of scientific, factual, linguistic and even iconoclastic approaches to the study of politics.

This last consideration may explain their persistence and popularity. It does not conceal the fact that they all overlook a fundamental truth. The earliest modern theories of the state originated in the closer association between the developing state and the developing community which became inevitable when it was discovered that power must be shared between the two. The concept of the sovereignty of the ruler was at the outset an essential ingredient of these theories for a good reason. When it became one essential feature of political society, this division of power or this collaboration of forces did not dim the importance of another—the need to ensure the effective exercise of power. The function of the concept of sovereignty was to provide the only possible compromise formula by which this primary need could still be met despite the development of this unavoidable association. As the community became still more complex the concept of the sovereignty of the ruler was challenged by the thesis of the sovereignty of the people and even, later, by the thesis that the state was dispensable. These arguments could not meet this primary need, however, the more so as the growing complexity of the community was only serving to emphasize the importance of the state. On both of these accounts the only recourse was to preserve sovereignty in the society by tightening still further the association between the state and the community at the expense of incurring greater complexity also in the character, the forms and procedures and the conception of the state. It is safe to say that, far from seeking to destroy it, the central developments of modern times in that direction—the rise of legislatures, the extension of suffrages, the introduction of representation and the insertion of constitutional features into the composition or the basis of executive organs—have been produced by the fundamental need to preserve the sovereignty of the state, as the pre-condition of effective action in and by the community, against the growth in modern political societies of other imperative but nevertheless less basic needs.

In just the same way, the effect of these central developments has been not to render the theory that the state is sovereign an unnecessary or inaccurate theory, and not to bring about a situation in which this assumption is no longer regularly accepted. It has been only to make it less necessary to insist in normal political circumstances, and less easy to perceive in normal political circumstances, that the operation of an advanced political society depends upon this thesis which remains the basic working assumption in internal no less than in international politics.

It is not to be expected that the application of any single political thesis, even that which attributes sovereignty to the state, will not sometimes result in controversy or even inconsistency in modern conditions: the internal structure of the modern political society is so complex. This complexity has so much further increased in most recent times that earlier formulations of this thesis have necessarily broken down. A thesis which derives its *raison d'être* from the relations between the community and the state must ever be reformulated as those relations change. As Austin above a century ago could no longer subscribe to all of Bodin's arguments, or even to some of Hobbes's, so contemporary theorists may justly take exception to Austin's belief that the law is what the sovereign commands and that what the sovereign does not command is not the law. But so long as the relations between the community and the state continue to require regulation—so long, for example, as Austin remains correct to the extent that no political and legal system can function unless it is ultimately rooted in the existence of coercive machinery which can enforce compliance with its decrees—there will be need for the concept of sovereignty, which authorizes and justifies the regulating authority.

It is for this reason that many recent criticisms of the concept have been only criticisms of some detailed formulation of it which leave the concept itself untouched; that the attempts to dismiss it altogether have been made by political theorists concerned to question whether the relations of the state and the community ought to be the ultimate source of political authority; that except within incompletely developed political societies, as in those which remain segmentary or those which are suspended at the federal stage, these attempts have been forced to rely on abnormal contingencies and improbable examples. And it is not for nothing that these attempts have obtained no support as yet either from lawyers and politicians, whose business is to operate the existing political framework, or from the mass of men whose interest is that it should continue to perform its function.

SUGGESTIONS FOR FURTHER READING

Chapter I

ADCOCK, F. E., "Greek and Macedonian Kingship", in *Proceedings of the British Academy* (1953).

DE JOUVENAL, B., *Sovereignty* (1957).

EISENSTADT, S. N., *The Political Systems of Empires* (1963).

FALLERS, L. A. (Ed.), *The King's Men; Leadership and Status in Buganda on the Eve of Independence* (1964).

FINLEY, M. I., *The World of Odysseus* (1956).

FORTES, M., and EVANS PRITCHARD, E. E., *African Political Systems* (1958).

GOODY, JACK, "Feudalism in Africa", in *Journal of African History*, Vol. IV, No. 1 (1963).

MACIVER, R. M. and PAGE, C. H., *Society* (1959).

MAIR, LUCY, *Primitive Government* (1962).

RICHARDS, AUDREY, I., "African Kings and their Royal Relatives", in *Journal of the Royal Anthropological Society*, Vol. 91, Part 2 (1961).

SCHAPERA, I., *Government and Politics in Tribal Societies* (1951).

SOUTHALL, A. W., *Alur Society* (1956), especially pp. 238–60.

Chapter II

ADCOCK, F. E., "Greek and Macedonian Kingship", in *Proceedings of the British Academy* (1953).

BARKER, ERNEST (Ed.,), *Aristotle's Politics* (1946).

BARKER, ERNEST, *Greek Political Theory. Plato and his Predecessors* (1947).

BÉRANGER, JEAN, *Recherches sur l'aspect idéologique du principat* (1953).

BAUDIN, L., *A Socialist Empire: the Incas of Peru* (1961).

FINLEY, M. I., *The Ancient Greeks* (1963).

FRYE, R. N., *The Heritage of Persia* (1962).

HAMMOND, MASON, *The Antonine Monarchy* (1959).

JONES, A. H. M., *Athenian Democracy* (1957).

JONES, A. H. M., *Studies in Roman Government and Law* (1960).

KAERST, JULIUS, *Geschichte der Hellenismus* (1926).

KOEBNER, R., *Empire* (1961).

SPELLMAN, JOHN W., *The Political Theory of Ancient India: a Study of Kingship from the Earliest Times to c.A.D. 300* (1964).

Chapter III

BAUMER, F. L., *The Early Tudor Theory of Kingship* (1938).

BAYNES, NORMAN, H., *The Byzantine Empire* (1925).

BLOCH, MARC, *Les rois thaumaturges* (1924).

BLOCH, MARC, *Feudal Society* (Eng. trans., 1961).

CHABOD, F., *Machiavelli and the Renaissance* (Eng. trans., 1958).

ELTON, G. R., *The Tudor Constitution* (1960).

FIGGIS, J. N., *The Divine Right of Kings* (1965 edn., with an introduction by G. R. Elton).

FRANKLIN, J. H., *Jean Bodin and the Sixteenth-century Revolution in the Methodology of Law and History* (1963).

GIERKE, OTTO, *Political Theories of the Middle Age* (Eng. trans. by F. W. Maitland, 1900).

GIERKE, OTTO, *Natural Law and the Theory of Society* (Eng. trans. by Ernest Barker, 1934).

GREENLEAF, W. H., *Order, Empiricism and Politics* (1964).

GRUNEBAUM, G. E., *Medieval Islam* (2nd Edn., 1953).

KANTOROWICZ, E., *The King's Two Bodies* (1957).

KERN, F., *Kingship and Law in the Middle Ages* (Eng. trans. by S. B. Chrimes, 1939).

KOEBNER, R., *Empire* (1961).

McILWAIN, C. H., *The Growth of Political Thought in the West* (1932).

MEINECKE, F., *Machiavellism* (Eng. trans., 1957).

MORRIS, C., *Political Thought in England, Tyndale to Hooker* (1953).

OSTROGORSKY, G. A., *History of the Byzantine State* (1956).

POST, GAINES, *Studies in Medieval Legal Thought* (1964).

RAAB, F., *The English Face of Machiavelli* (1964).

REESE, M. M., *The Cease of Majesty* (1961).

REYNOLDS, BEATRICE, *Proponents of Limited Monarchy in Sixteenth-century France* (1931).

RIDOLFI, R., *Life of Niccolò Machiavelli* (Eng. trans., 1963).

ROSENTHAL, E. I. J., *Political Thought in Medieval Islam* (1958).

RUNCIMAN, S., *Byzantine Civilisation* (1933).

SCHRAMM, P. E., *A History of the English Coronation* (1937).

ULLMANN, W., *Principles of Government and Politics in the Middle Ages* (1961).

ULLMANN, W., "Reflections on the Medieval Empire" in *Transactions of the Royal Historical Society*, 5th Series, Vol. XIV (1964).

WILKS, M., *The Problem of Sovereignty in the Later Middle Ages* (1963).

Chapter IV

BARKER, ERNEST, *Political Thought in England from Herbert Spencer to the Present Day* (1915).

DÉRATHÉ, R., *Jean Jacques Rousseau et la science politique de son temps* (1950).

DICEY, A. V., *Introduction to the Study of the Law of the Constitution* (10th edn., 1959).

DICEY, A. V., *Lectures on the Relation between Law and Public Opinion in England during the Nineteenth Century* (2nd edn., 1914).

FIGGIS, J. N., *The Divine Right of Kings* (1956 edn. with an introduction by G. R. Elton).

GIERKE, OTTO, *Natural Law and the Theory of Society* (Eng. trans. by Ernest Barker, 1934).

GIERKE, OTTO, *The Development of Political Theory* (Eng. trans., 1939).

GOOCH, G. P., *English Democratic Ideas in the Seventeenth Century* (2nd edn., 1927).

JUDSON, MARGARET A., *The Crisis of the Constitution* (1949).

LASKI, HAROLD J., *Political Thought in England from Locke to Bentham* (1920).

MERRIAM, C. E., *History of the Theory of Sovereignty since Rousseau* (1900).

MOSSE, G. L., *The Struggle for Sovereignty in England* (1950).

POCOCK, J. G. A., *The Ancient Constitution and the Feudal Law* (1957).

SALMON, J. H. M., *The French Religious Wars in English Political Thought* (1959).

SKINNER, QUENTIN, "History and Ideology in the English Revolution", in *The Historical Journal*, Vol. VIII (1965).

WATKINS, J. W. N., *Hobbes's System of Ideas* (1965).

WESTON, CORINNE COMSTOCK, *English Constitutional Theory and the House of Lords, 1566–1832* (1965).

Chapter V

ARON, R., *Paix et guerre entre les nations* (1962).

DEHIO, L., *Precarious Balance, 1494–1945* (Eng. trans., 1963).

DUPUIS, C., *Le droit des gens et les rapports des grands puissants avec les autres états* (1921).

DE VISSCHER, C., *Theory and Reality in International Law* (Eng. trans., 1957).

GALLOUÉDEC-GENUYS, FRANÇOISE, *Le prince selon Fénelon* (1963).

GIERKE, OTTO, *Natural Law and the Theory of Society* (Eng. trans. by Ernest Barker, 1934).

HINSLEY, F. H., *Power and the Pursuit of Peace* (1963).

LAUTERPACHT, H., *Private Law Sources and Analogies of International Law* (1927).

LAUTERPACHT, H., "The Grotian Tradition in International Law", in *British Year Book of International Law*, Vol. XXIII (1946).

MAINE, SIR HENRY, *Ancient Law* (new edn., 1930).

MAINE, SIR HENRY, *International Law* (1888).

MATTINGLY, G., *Renaissance Diplomacy* (1955).

MEINECKE, F., *Machiavellism* (Eng. trans., 1957).

NUSSBAUM, A., *A Concise History of the Law of Nations* (1954).

POST, GAINES, *Studies in Medieval Legal Thought* (1964).

SCHWARZENBERGER, G., *Power Politics* (3rd edn., 1964).

SMITH, H. A., *Great Britain and the Law of Nations* (2 vols., 1932, 1935).

TAYLOR, A. J. P., *The Struggle for Mastery in Europe, 1848–1918* (1954).

ZELLER, GASTON, "Rois de France candidats à l'Empire", in *Revue historique*, 1934; reprinted in the author's *Aspects de la politique française sous l'ancien régime* (1964).

Chapter VI

HART, H. L. A., *The Concept of Law* (1961).

HERZ, JOHN, *International Politics and the Atomic Age* (1959).

KELSEN, H., *General Theory of Law and the State* (Eng. trans., 1954).

KELSEN, H., *Law and Peace* (1942).

LASKI, HAROLD J., *The Grammar of Politics* (1941).

LLOYD, DENNIS, *The Idea of Law* (1964).

MACIVER, R. M., *The Modern State* (1926).

PENROSE, E. F., *The Revolution in International Affairs* (1965).

REES, W. J., "The Theory of Sovereignty Restated", in *Philosophy, Politics and Society* (ed. P. Laslett, 1956).

WADE, H. W. R., "The Basis of Legal Sovereignty", in *The Cambridge Law Journal* (November, 1955).

WRIGHT, PHILIP QUINCY, *Mandates under the League of Nations* (1930).

ADDENDA

The following books have appeared while the present work was in the press—

Chapter II

LEVI, MARIO ATTILIO, *Political Power in the Ancient World* (Eng. trans., 1965).

Chapter III

ULLMANN, W., *A History of Political Thought: The Middle Ages* (1965).

INDEX